ADVANCE PRAISE

Analysis and analytics presupposes a razor-sharp mind that can manipulate complex data sets to make sense out of chaos. It also assumes an ability to bring the right data to the discussion. Arindam does both with brutal honesty, to ensure that information and data never get buried under opinions and anecdotes.

As management education takes centre stage, acquires a halo and gets deified, the need to apply analytical rigour to the management of management education has only increased. Arindam helps us discard preconceived notions and in a systematic manner encourages the reader to pierce through the halo.

Chef Arindam gives us the perfect recipe of analysis, anticipation and acumen peppered with a dash of hard-talking honesty. Bon appétit.

—Niteen Bhagwat
Executive Director, DraftFCB-Ulka & CEO, Asterii
Analytics, Mumbai, India

Professor Banerjee has written a brilliant tour de force on management education, making the case for teaching rigorous approaches to business management and debunking the notion that it is merely placement mechanism to serve companies. A thought-changing book, written in a lucid and engaging writing style, which develops a practical 'Anticipation-Transformation-Money' (ATM) framework.

—Dr Suresh Divakar
Vice President, Bristol-Myers Squibb,
New Jersey, USA

Why some organizations fail but some succeed? Why some fail to sustain their success story but some others can? These questions are as intriguing as why some nations are rich and some are poor. Scores of books are written on this topic but most are anecdotal in nature. In this delightfully readable book, Banerjee develops a convincing thesis with verve, grounded in scientific management principles and generalizable across contexts.

—**Tathagata Bandyopadhyay**
Professor, Indian Institute of Management, Ahmedabad

Armed with long years of academic and consulting experience, Dr Banerjee weaves together a treatise on 'Utilitarian' Management, sharpening the theories that are taught today in elite business schools, and modelling them to fit into the practical business world. This book will help you at any stage of life that you are in: as a student, it will help answer your fledgling questions; as a sceptic, 'been there, done that', it will let you think, re-think and hopefully, re-visit your ideas.

—**Pranav Bhattacharya**
Manager, Business Intelligence Management, Capgemini
Financial Services, Pune

There are many books in the market that claim to provide a practitioner's view of management principles. However, they mostly lack the depth of academic rigor or their ability to translate the same for meaning use. This is an ideal book that works as a compendium of practical management gyan (experience) written with strong theoretical underpinning. To the casual reader, this book may look impressive because of sheer variety of topics it covers, but to the practitioners of management the book provides depth of detail and creates an integrated view of decision-making process of organizations.

—**Dheeraj Awasthy**
Senior Banking Professional, Bangalore

A truly original piece of work that structures management thought in a unique and understandable manner for mass consumption. Prof. Banerjee has successfully attempted to make seemingly 'hard to acquire' management principles in a simple and lucid writing style that benefits one and all. The 'ATM' framework which he has proposed is a worthwhile piece for organizations to recognize, although the author rightfully qualifies this with the difficulty that many face in adhering to it. Interestingly, the book also positions the role of quantitative analysis in strategic decision making in a manner that the reader is not blinded, but is encouraged to use them rationally and appropriately. All in all, a very enjoyable book which serves as a useful reference for all practicing managers to revisit their fundamental management acumen periodically.

—**Vivek Gupta**
Chief Innovation Officer, Essex Lake Group LLC, NJ

MANAGEMENT ESSENTIALS

MANAGEMENT ESSENTIALS

A Recipe for Business Success

Arindam Banerjee

SAGE | Response Business Books

www.sagepublications.com

Los Angeles • London • New Delhi • Singapore • Washington DC

First published in 2013 by

SAGE Response
B1/I-1 Mohan Cooperative Industrial Area
Mathura Road, New Delhi 110 044, India

SAGE Publications Inc
2455 Teller Road
Thousand Oaks, California 91320, USA

SAGE Publications Ltd
1 Oliver's Yard, 55 City Road
London EC1Y 1SP, United Kingdom

SAGE Publications Asia-Pacific Pte Ltd
33 Pekin Street
#02-01 Far East Square
Singapore 048763

Published by Vivek Mehra for SAGE Publications India Pvt Ltd, typeset in 11/15 Century Schoolbook by RECTO Graphics, Delhi, and printed at Saurabh Printers Pvt Ltd.

Library of Congress Cataloging-in-Publication Data

Banerjee, Arindam.
    Management essentials : a recipe for business success / Arindam Banerjee.
        pages cm
    Includes bibliographical references.
    1. Management. I. Title.
    HD31.B26   658—dc23   2013   013020380

ISBN: 978-81-321-1103-0 (PB)

The SAGE Team: Sachin Sharma, Shreya Lall, Rajib Chatterjee and Rajinder Kaur

To my father, who did not get to see many of the fruits of his paternal affection.

To my daughter, Antara and son, Dhruv, who generously gave up some of their quality time with their 'Baba', for me to aggressively pursue my academic quest.

To the indefatigable spirit of the participants in the various academic and corporate training and research programmes that I have taught over the past 14 years being part of the faculty at IIM Ahmedabad. I have learnt a lot from their diverse experience and sharp acumen.

Thank you for choosing a SAGE product! If you have any comment, observation or feedback, I would like to personally hear from you. Please write to me at contactceo@sagepub.in

—Vivek Mehra, Managing Director and CEO,
SAGE Publications India Pvt Ltd, New Delhi

Bulk Sales

SAGE India offers special discounts for purchase of books in bulk. We also make available special imprints and excerpts from our books on demand.

For orders and enquiries, write to us at

Marketing Department
SAGE Publications India Pvt Ltd
B1/I-1, Mohan Cooperative Industrial Area
Mathura Road, Post Bag 7
New Delhi 110044, India
E-mail us at marketing@sagepub.in

Get to know more about SAGE, be invited to SAGE events, get on our mailing list. Write today to marketing@sagepub.in

This book is also available as an e-book.

CONTENTS

LIST OF ILLUSTRATIONS

FIGURES

TABLES

BOXES

FOREWORD

There are many books in the field of management; at the same time, a favourite lament of many a practitioner is about lack of one that can bridge the chasm of academic thought and practice in an enterprise. *Haven't we all heard ourselves or our esteemed colleagues in organizations speak: 'This may be good for the books but it doesn't work here.'*

In such a context it is a delight to see a book that is making a significant attempt at an integrative approach, blending thought and application. And I cannot think of a better academician than Professor Arindam Banerjee to write such a book, as he has a remarkable ability to transcend theory and delve into management practice with élan at short notice.

Over the decade that I have known Arindam, I have always seen him passionately advocate sound management theory to anchor thinking and to make informed decisions. He sees analysis and decision-making as Yin and Yang of managing an enterprise and has healthy respect for managerial acumen in creating a successful business organization. The basics tenets of this book are grounded in the same principles of thinking reinforced with relevant anecdotes and simple wisdoms.

A distinguishing thought brought forward in the book is that of brand as an outcome of managerial acumen and action. Using a simple yet sticky acronym like 'ATM', the book helps the reader in keeping the managerial reality of a highly volatile and uncertain environment in focus, while planning and taking action for long-term success of the organization.

Wikipedia mentions garnish as an embellishment that may give an added or contrasting flavour. Using this culinary metaphor in his final chapter, Arindam has innovatively provided an additional flavour to the book. Whether it is his dispassionate plea to 'not hire consultants' or serving portions of witty sermons using well-chosen quotes on 'good habits of management', his deeply held convictions stand out. It is laudable that he has openly highlighted the perils of dependency on consultants despite being one himself.

In conclusion, reading this book would be a worthwhile investment of time and it can prove to be a great aid to both students and practitioners of management.

Anupam Sirbhaiya
Country Manager (India)
Center for Creative Leadership

PREFACE

WHY THE NEED TO REVISIT BASIC MANAGEMENT PRINCIPLES?

Having spent many years in the business school, first as a student, then as a researcher and, more recently, as a teacher and professor of management science, I am now tempted to pen down my own thoughts concisely about all the knowledge and wisdom that I think gets transacted in many reputed institutions of business education. While they are useful for providing the building blocks of running enterprises of many kinds, mainstream business education in today's time is somewhat consigned to a strange mysticism that makes it both aspirational and hard to reach for people. At the same time, it is also poohpoohed by many for its supposed lack of application. The latter group comprises a motley bunch of people, partly successful in enterprise and who have most probably graduated from the portals of these esteemed institutions, which they now decree as impractical in their impartation of management thought.

I must begin this discourse with some well-deserved plaudits for this sector of education. The amount of furore that management 'science' or 'arts' has created in India today is truly remarkable. This is a reflection of the maturity and critical stock of intellect that exists in the society today to argue vigorously the various nuances of this relatively new field of knowledge.

I see three strong segments of opinion makers in this field. Pardon me for making a high-level generalization— there certainly would be other well-considered viewpoints that exist in nooks and crannies of the topology, but for the sake of simplicity, I would implore that we keep them aside for due consideration on another day. I wish to describe the three segments that I would like to consider over here:

1. The supposed puritans who adorn the portals of branded business schools of India. I happen to be part of this segment given my over-a-decade–long association with one such school.
2. The practitioners of business management, both with formal and non-formal education who have picked up additionally the art of resolving real-life organizational issues.
3. The retired practitioners who have presumably developed and gathered the relevant knowledge of managing organizations through their experiences in their professional life and are now ready to impart the same to the future generation.

While all three professional groups in the aforementioned business domain have similar intent, i.e., to further the knowledge of management principles, I must make some distinction between the methods that they have adopted, something that has steadily increased my wariness about the future of this stream of education in India.

THE CURRENT OPINION MAKERS IN MANAGEMENT EDUCATION

First, I must start with the description of my own seg-ment—the 'puritans'. For a fact, we puritans have domi-nated the business-school education over the past 50 odd years. A few of us, the premier and oldest institutions in this domain, have recently celebrated our golden jubilee anniversary of existence. From their initiation and to some extent till date, these institutions remain coveted institu-tions for middle-class India for admission to one of their many programmes. The attraction is more towards the 'reputable' and vocationally driven training programmes, also known as the Post Graduate Programmes (PGPs). Over the years, there has been a surge in the demand for such primary-level vocational trainings at these institutes, although the esteem of these institutions in all other academic areas such as thought leadership, academic research and advanced training and retooling has been steadily declining. Part of this decline can be attributed to environmental factors such as increased competition from global institutions; however, it would be unwise to ignore the erosion of competency within these institutes.

Many a debate has been initiated in this realm, regard-ing what ails the business school of today in India. The well-articulated fact that faculty competency is declining due to wage disparities across sectors that have made resources scarce in the education sector has been stated oftentimes. But there appear to be some fundamental fault lines which may be stymieing the process of creating academic excellence.

Theory enhancement and excellence in academic enterprise may require cooperative leadership amongst institutions at the top to foster a healthy knowledge enhancement climate. These have to do with academic pride, something broader than what mundane hygiene factors such as pay parity can achieve. Unfortunately, premier Indian business schools were established in spirit to drive primary-level vocational training courses, which they have achieved reasonably well and with aggressive competitiveness amongst themselves. Even in today's time, most institutes would agree that their flagship programme is the PGP (or its equivalent). However, that itself is the seed of non-cooperative competition amongst institutes which impedes any significant intellectual activity, especially in times when proficiency in the faculty is on the decline.

I will park the debate on institutional competency over here for the while, while I shift my focus on the practitioners. I think this is a mixed bunch and certainly compliments many of them who are doing an excellent job of mixing theory and practice together to create knowledge that may be more grounded to the context, but at the same time, has far-reaching positive results for everybody across the management domain. Kudos to them and I do hope this trend continues.

However, I must also refer to a counter-trend in this domain that really rubbishes all theory (or most of it) as exotic 'mind play' and relies primarily on the 'tricks of the trade'—a vast plethora of rules that managers have picked up over years of practice (thumb rules) that is handed over from one generation to another. While not ignoring the importance of practice ploys, something that academic theory may never be able to comprehensively and rationally validate, the trend towards pooh-poohing formalized management education as just a 'feather on the cap', necessary for getting a head start in one's professional life and not much more, is very alarming. One may question the relevance of current management theory in practice, which is the genesis of further enquiry and research, but questioning the relevance of theory in general can best be stated as disastrous in the long run. This segment of theory-baiters appears to be growing over time and is now more so a trend in the management realm than anywhere else.

The disturbing element is the fact that neither industry nor the academia is seriously considering the implications of such trends. A fallout of this trend has been the relegation of business schools to being largely a route to seeking good industry placements by students, and therefore ensuring that they are able to window-dress their resumes according to the expectations of their prospective employers. Employers, on the other hand, appear to be looking for a stock of talent from business schools (assuming that the better ones would naturally find their way to the branded schools), not really caring as much for the training imparted at these educational programmes. In many instances, the process of learning actually is supposed to begin at the workplace, as it is stated by them, which is preceded by unlearning some of the 'impractical' theory imparted during the academic sessions.

An obvious consequence of this trend is the creation in recent times of the third segment—many of them are retirees from practice, who have accumulated a vast reserve of knowledge and have the confidence to bestow it on the next generation (in some cases for revenue generation). Some of them vehemently contradict the formal business school curriculum with their own brand of practice-based wisdom. Many such business education enterprises have become vibrant operations in the past decade attracting students hungry for a business degree, but not having the fortitude to make it to the more established academic programmes of the country.

I want to seek restraint on this kind of enterprise. For reasons more than one, formal educational curriculum is a serious enough business which requires a certain amount of rigorous application of collegiate enterprise. If practice-based curriculum is inadvertently recognized as a healthy substitute for the shortfalls of an academic programme devised for imparting formal education, we will be shifting our knowledge base from scientific theorems to anecdotal paradigms. While there has been a debate for many years on the need for strong anecdotal support for conceptualizing theory in management for good reasons, it would be hard to defend a move towards building theory solely based on examples that many practitioners tend to preach.

There is some evidence in history that supports this thinking though. The original intention of setting up national-level institutions in India to impart vocational oriented business management education was more to provide a 'top up' complement to a fundamental training imparted at the universities. The thinking was that a well-trained engineer, scientist or liberal arts graduate would require some appreciation on the principles of running enterprises, a complementary set of skills to the original training that they had undergone in physical or social sciences or liberal arts. That may, in part, be the reason for the genesis of the practice orientation of business management education.

The evolution of the MBA schools in other parts of the world, over the years, has been somewhat different. While the practice-oriented programmes are still in vogue, business education has become more academic, and theoretical research has become imperative like any other discipline. Hence, major business schools around the world are driving cutting-edge research, which need not necessarily be context specific, and are motivated largely to develop more scientifically grounded principles of the subject that can be generalized across contexts. Hence, the trend in business education too is moving away from practice to theory construction, with a firm belief that strong theory would drive best practice of the future.

That said, no one can circumvent the discomfort that industry has towards many Indian business school impartations. This discord stems from the academic institutions' inability to contextualize their delivery to the real world. In the process, the output has steadily been perceived to be of mere baseline value.

Over the years, I have been intrigued by this phenomenon and fear that as an educationist, my lot will slowly lose its primacy for very genuine reasons. We have been 'sitting in our ivory towers' for long. While the idea of book writing never crossed my mind until now, I have now found it necessary to document my thinking about management concepts and their relevance in my own meandering way, lest I forget it myself. This is my first attempt to reorganize my thoughts—not forgetting the theoretical construct of management, but at the same time clambering down to the ground floor to deal with the reality while making the knowledge realistic and for mass appeal. In the process, I may miss out on the exotic elements of management thought. However, if I can cover the foundations for the new era, others may follow to build the subsequent floors to the building.

THE TENOR OF THIS MANUSCRIPT

In conclusion, I would like to reiterate my intent with regard to writing this manuscript. I am a great believer of theory in any realm because it provides an anchor to build a firm foundation for application. Without strong theoretical underpinnings, applications will move around in 'Brownian motion'. At the same time, management as a field of academic pursuit is facing some of its greatest challenges in India today. The question is about its realism to the context. In their pursuit for realism, many are advocating the need to set aside theory and believe in 'best practices' alone. While the latter has its merits, steering clear of theoretical foundations is grossly risky for the development of knowledge and new discovery, which is generalizable over contexts. This manuscript is more of an attempt to rejig management thought to make it more realistic without sacrificing on the strong foundations of rationality. At the same time, it is at best a translation of existing theory into more realistic parlance. I claim no credit for expanding the boundaries of management theory beyond its existing perimeter of familiarity.

The rest of this manuscript describes some commonplace management principles in simplistic parlance. The plausible readership for this may be someone with at least a basic exposure to management practice or theory, just so that they are familiar with some of the terminologies and assumptions that have been used in the course of the description. I have tried to make a unified view for many of the seemingly abstract and disparate issues that are discussed and practised in the real world. In this process, I would hope to have covered most of the dimensions of critical importance in general management of any normal for-profit enterprise. The organization of the chapters is as follows: I will begin with providing a general management principle for successfully running typical organizations. The approach is no different than describing the 'recipe' for making an Indian curry (available from a cookbook). The following chapters (chapters 2, 3 and 4) will describe the 'ingredients' required to make the curry. I shall then (in Chapter 5) describe the role of management 'analysis' in facilitating the right support infrastructure to run organizations successfully. All good cooks require a suitable and well-equipped kitchen to apply their culinary skills successfully and it is no different in the management world. Finally, I will close the discourse

(Chapter 6) with an exposition on 'branding'. In my opinion, it is the climax of all good or bad management practices, unlike some popular mainstream notions. I would like to clarify some issues with respect to popularly held views on branding. Additionally, all good curries are topped with some garnish (Chapter 7) and I will leave the reader with some stray 'words of acumen' that I could not include successfully in the main body of my text.

ACKNOWLEDGEMENTS

I would like to acknowledge the significant role, over the years, of my colleagues at IIM Ahmedabad, especially Bibek Banerjee, Tathagata Bandyopadhyay, Devanath Tirupati and Pankaj Chandra with whom I have worked in many co-created academic programmes that have proved beneficial in providing relevant inputs to write this manuscript. I am indebted to them for the numerous intellectual parleys that we have had during our collaboration, which has sharpened my thinking on various theoretical issues in management science.

A special thanks to many of my corporate partners who provided the stage for me to hone my management principles into practice. Among them, the longest and productive relationships have been with Anupam Sirbhaiya at Tata Management Training Centre, Scott Williams at HSBC and earlier at Mitchell Madison Group, Dheeraj Awasthy and Vivek Gupta, who were doctoral students at IIM Ahmedabad and later became very reliable industry partners, R. Balasubramanian at TNS Global Market Research, Suresh Divakar at Kraft Foods and Mitchell Madison Group and Uday Kumar at ACNielsen and at HSBC.

I have to recognize the enormous role that Prachi Acharya, Academic Associate in the Marketing Area at IIM Ahmedabad, played in providing very useful research support and pointed critique of an earlier draft of the manuscript and for some very effective ideas regarding the organization of the manuscript. My sincere thanks to her for her timely and cheerful support.

I have to thank my extended family for constantly encouraging me to successfully complete this venture.

Lastly, I must highlight the 'behind the scene' but very inspiring role played by my wife, Tanushri. It was on the basis of her incessant exhortation that I pieced together all the stray pieces of learning acquired during my ongoing academic life at IIM Ahmedabad and plunged into this pursuit. Besides ensuring time and space during a particular trying phase in our professional lives for me to pursue this activity, as a peer in the management profession, she has been instrumental in giving her share of ideas and critique which shaped this manuscript.

This writing initiative has been supported partly by the financial grant provided by the Research & Publications Office of IIM Ahmedabad.

One

EFFECTIVE MANAGEMENT PHILOSOPHY

The Rationale*

THE RECIPE FOR A GREAT 'MANAGEMENT' CURRY

Managing an organization successfully long term is like running a marathon. You need lasting power and the right timing to deploy your strength to race ahead of the pack at the critical juncture. It is very much unlike a 100-metre race where a short but tremendous burst of energy can help attain you to your objective.

There have been countless occasions in my B-school academic life when I have been confronted with a very simple question—what sustains successful organizations? Believe it or not, every time I have struggled to provide a convincing answer.

Inevitably, my discomfort is shared by many, although there are numerous suggestions of the need for management principles such as efficiency and prudence, innovative climate, flexible organization and strong and foresighted leadership, customer focus and

---

*An earlier version appeared as 'The Science of Creating Business Acumen', *TMTC Journal of Management*, December 2010, by the author.

effective stakeholder relationship management, which steer respected organizations to greater heights. In spite of the truism associated with these principles, many of us remain unsure about the criterion for using them— are they all needed in equal doses in every organization or do they vary across circumstances? A relatively safe alternative would be to bet on the latter, although it still does not address our simple question with which we started this discourse.

Doubtlessly, the principles stated here are traits that better-managed organizations pick up—there are many case studies of champions in the corporate world that have built or imbibed such healthy habits which are inscribed in various management chronicles over the years. However, one wonders why management principles keep changing over time with changes in the environment. Lurking behind these 'healthy' practices, there may be a shred of a scientific theorem that determines success of business organizations, never mind the nature of the context that may change from time to time.

It is somewhat like unravelling the 'practice of good cooking', no matter what is being cooked. Just like what Virgin does from selling 'air travel' to 'soft drinks' with equal chutzpah and verve or our very own TATA does from selling robust 'trucks' to a pack of 'salt' with equal élan and trust!

UNRAVELLING THE 'SCIENCE'

Oftentimes in my mission to unravel this 'mystery' of good management science in my classroom conversations,

I have begun the discussion with elementary questions, such as *(a)* What is a manager paid for? and *(b)* How does she/he achieve this and sustain it over time?

The discussion usually veers around the dynamics of the outside environment and the need to forecast well and control external environment parameters 'as best as is possible' in the long term. But it is a known fact that the forecasting function is usually 'wildly' stochastic (indeterminate), where the unpredictability can run as high as predicting the weather conditions of Ahmedabad city for the next 10 days in advance. A significant part of the manager's effort goes in sensing what may be the business conditions in the days to come, since much of our internal 'preparedness' to weather the new business climate depends on it.

The fact of the matter is that we almost never succeed anywhere close to predicting anything right. Much of the rest of the manager's time goes into deciding the best way to react to such 'unforeseen' changes in the environment and ensuring that the health of the organization is not impaired because of 'too late' or 'inflexible' reaction.

Life is a cobweb. The lines cross at funny angles. Whether you're successful or not doesn't depend on how good your plans are especially those five year strategic plans business schools teach. Success depends on how you react to unexpected opportunities.

—Ross Perot

Even established organizations such as Xerox, HP, IBM, Merck, Texas Instruments, Disney and Boeing went through such rough weather at some point in their history and recovered. In an article in *Inc.*,[1] Jim Collins compares 3M with Norton. He states:

> 3M began life as a failed mine and could not pay its first president a salary for 11 years. Yet it grew into one of the most innovative companies in history, eventually branching into more than 60,000 new products. In contrast, Norton began life with a revolutionary new grinding wheel that propelled the company to spectacular early growth. Yet Norton became a stodgy old-line company, with no reputation for sustained innovation.

The business world's topmost attention is paid to this eternal struggle to predict the future. Additionally, the fact that it is largely untenable provides a buttress to the organization to react suitably and, to the greatest extent possible, seamlessly to changing contours of the outside topography.

Interestingly, while we may rue the fact that the outside world is hard to predict and control to a great degree, it is important to realize that this element of unpredictability is oftentimes the root cause of the need for good managerial talent in the organization. In a lighter vein, some introspection will reveal that it is best that the future does not reveal itself anywhere close to perfection, for that would mitigate the need for intelligent managerial interventions to run organizations. Loss in uncertainty in the business environment could result in organizations being programmed in a preset fashion to react optimally to a perfectly predicted future. Hopefully, such 'eventualities' will not show up anytime soon.

---

[1] Jim Collins, 'Building Companies to Last', *Inc.* (Special Issue: May: The State of Small Business, 1995). Available online at http:/www.inc.com/magazine/19950515/2692.html

THE FORMULATION OF THE 'SCIENCE'

Most of us have heard the virtues of value creation for customers to reap long-term profits. What is relatively unknown is the path to creating value for customers' profitably. In today's context, a lot of emphasis is being given to the role of innovation and creativity in the value creation process. The argument posed is that new ideas that create path-breaking products and service models and that are relevant to consumers are needed and processes ought to be developed to harness such ideas continuously. Putting it in the words of IBM CEO Samuel J. Palmisano: 'The way you will thrive in this environment is by innovating—innovating in technologies, innovating in strategies, innovating in business models.' It is undoubtedly a prudent investment for organizations, but value in a competitive environment is not just about innovation, but 'smart' innovation. By this I mean that it is important for organizations to innovate as described earlier, but they must also do enough to ensure that such innovations (if they create impact) are less likely to be emulated by the competitor, even if the latter wants to.

Hence, innovations which create 'true' value are the ones that are: *(a)* relevant for customers and *(b)* difficult for competitors to copy almost 'instantaneously'.

$$\text{Value} = \frac{\text{Benefits Delivered Relative to Competition}}{\text{Price at which It Is Delivered}}$$

One of the many avenues for value creation is to look within your organization to identify dimensions (people, processes and assets) that can be translated to value drivers in such a way that may be superior compared to the competitor's capabilities. Most successful businesses seem to have managed this strategy well, at least during the period they remained successful.

The last issue about value creation is the one about scope. Value creation can happen due to innovation in product, technology or service dimension that provides additional but relevant benefits to customers. Value creation may also manifest itself in the form of lower 'cost to customer' through promotions and price reductions. The complication with this is that price-reduction strategy is imminently copyable by all competitors in the short run and hence, if an organization has to harness long-term benefits due to low cost, it must ensure that it remains one of the lowest cost producers in the market (efficiency in delivery has to be high). That would ensure that it is able to beat all other competitors successfully by having the ability to lower price (without making loss) more than anybody else. Retailing giant Walmart is a stunning illustration for the same. Others like the Korean giants Samsung and LG with enormous scales in their manufacturing facilities and unmatched efficiency in supply chains are practically dumping the world with their products.

Hence, in the value creation process, organizations must look within themselves, many a times, for dimensions of competency that can be transformed into relevant differentiators in their delivery process. The manifestations may be appropriately created, be it efficiency-led or benefit-led, depending upon the organization's competency profile relative to competition. A good example of such capability-led transformation has been evident in our retail industry in India (see Box 1.1).

BOX 1.1   Scaled Up Efficiency or Upscale Innovativeness

The neighbourhood grocer shuddered at the thought of that pervasive retail giant about to enter his city and who threatened to ruin his business. That depressing thought heralded the onslaught of organized retail chains with their professional ideas about how to do business and attract the Indian consumer and their purses. But, that was many years ago.

In the meanwhile, the professional retailers came in slowly but steadily and stayed, but so did the neighbourhood grocer. Necessity is the mother of invention, and it could not be exemplified better by the crusade of the 'mom and pop' (kirana) stores in India to survive the surge of large, purportedly professional retailers. In retrospect, the former's extinction was never in threat, nor will be, so long as their flexibility to adapt to changing environment remains intact.

So where did the big guys of retail find their forte? First, bigness has ensured a lower price line at the point of sale to the end consumer. An advantage they have acquired through leveraging their scale at the sourcing point of the supply chain. They may have also provided brighter, swankier and comfortable shopping environment to the customer, which has somewhat lost its sheen over the years. They have also enhanced product variety available at one place, something rarely encountered in the earlier times.

But that has not been enough to push the kirana guy out of the market. The retail boom, especially in food and grocery segment, has mainly taken up the slot that was earlier occupied by the Super Bazaars and the Apna Bazaars, albeit with a brighter and more cheerful façade and in larger numbers. The traditional strongholds of the kirana shops, the neighbourhood markets of the various residential localities of the city have remained more or less unchanged.

(Box 1.1 continued)

(Box 1.1 continued)

So, the dreaded substitution effect that was predicted has not been seen, instead, there has been significant traction towards building complementarities between the traditional and the new formats of food retailing. Kirana still rules a majority of the markets as the preferred point of purchase which is available at the 'street level'. Whereas, professionally organized retailing has found its space in attracting buyers for periodic planned purchases of high volume. But for a large number of the Indian consumers who are not financially equipped to take advantage of the savings provided by bulk purchases, the charm of shopping at the new age store has remained little more than a "window shopping" experience. In a few commercially savvy markets of the country, organized food and grocery retail outlets have worked out effectively as middlemen for the neighbourhood retail outlets, further building on the theory of complementarity.

This symbiotic characteristic of today's retailscape illustrates an important lesson for the management domain. It highlights the versatility of the minnow and its ability to reinvent itself, in the presence of formidable competition. While the latter primarily thrives on the dimension of efficiency and scale, smallness proves to be advantageous by providing the flexibility to adapt to match up to the changing requirements. Where else can one expect the readiness to serve, be it home delivery or short term credit or assistance in getting customized orders with alacrity but in the lakhs of kirana stores dotting our markets? All that, only for a small hike in the price charged. Large professional organizations with their elaborate internal controls to manage their scale will find it a tad more difficult to beat such 'guerrilla' tactics. This is a fundamental reason why flexibility and innovativeness tends to get restricted as the size of the organization increases.

Source: 'Adapt and Thrive', *Hindustan Times*, 24 April 2008.

Hence, in the value creation process, organizations must look within themselves, many a time, for dimensions of competency that can be transformed into relevant differentiators in their delivery process. The manifestations may be appropriately created, be it efficiency led or benefit led, depending on the organization's competency profile relative to competition.

HOW TO SUSTAIN CREATED VALUE?

Historically, a monopoly condition referred to a situation where the value creation was dominant and sustained and no other supplier could match up to supply similar or better output. Such monopolistic opportunities are few and far between in today's environment. Good innovation of product, process and service and its smart implementation do not ensure sustainability of a competitive position in the value creation process. Over time, it will inevitably be neutralized by competition, or by changes in the environment which bring in a new set of expectations from the consumer replacing old ones.

In the book *Closing the Execution Gap*,[2] author Richard Lepsinger states the example of Dell:

> Just as people can get stuck in a rut, so can businesses. Dell developed 'the Dell Way', and its reluctance to tread off of the beaten path cost it its customers. The company was able to attract customers to its website with low-cost offers that required the buyer to make additions in order to have the best computer (which meant the price would end up being more

---

[2]Richard Lepsinger, *Closing the Execution Gap: How Great Leaders and Their Companies Get Results* (USA: Pfeiffer & Company, 2010).

than the original low-cost offer). But when tons of affordable computers with all the bells and whistles that consumers wanted became readily available through other online outlets and retail stores, consumers didn't have to go to Dell to get a 'custom-made' computer.

Here's where Dell turned a problem into a huge problem. When its leaders realized they were losing business to competitors, they fell back on a practice that had always worked for them before: they cut costs to maintain market share. One area that suffered was customer service, which had originally been one of the company's biggest strengths.

Hence, we should be continuously looking for opportunities to create 'value', replacing old and worn-out opportunities, to provide sustenance for the competitive advantage which organizations require to remain healthy in the long run. It is important to emphasize the virtue of identifying (forecasting) 'right' opportunities to create 'value' in the future, for that links well with the exposition of the 'science' of creating 'business acumen' as described earlier in the chapter.

HOW CAN ORGANIZATIONS APPLY THE 'SCIENCE' TO REMAIN SUCCESSFUL IN THE LONG RUN (ATM)?

Managing a process of continuous and relevant innovation which provides unique and sustained advantage to the supplier is usually a tough proposition. Besides a long-term vision and competent people to execute it, this also requires the discipline of revisiting the organizational chemistry from time to time to check if its competencies are in line with the requirements for the future. If they are not, then a phase of replenishment of skills is necessary. What then may be a mix of processes (habits) that successful organizations should perhaps develop (pick up) to ensure their longevity? Our multiple in-class case analyses, discussions and research have helped us to cull out a few major ideas about such processes/'habits' which we list in the following sections.

Accurate Anticipation (A)

> Greatness is not a function of circumstance. Greatness, it turns out, is largely a matter of conscious choice and discipline.
> —Jim Collins

Accurate anticipation is perhaps the most critical and difficult habit to develop in organizations. Forecasting, as was earlier discussed, is a part of this more holistic discipline of anticipation. The longer the foresight and its accuracy, the better is the possibility of equipping the organization with the right competency in the long run. Most average performing business corporations remain closer to a state of extreme reactiveness to the environment (almost zero accuracy in anticipation). On the other hand, successful organizations are likely to have processes, discipline or just individuals in their top management cadre who are extremely foresighted and have steered their respective organizations successfully. No one can imagine a Reliance without Dhirubhai Ambani or an Infosys without Narayana Murthy or an Apple without Steve Jobs.

However, the unfortunate part is that many success stories (with exceptions) can be largely attributed to the farsightedness of specific individuals who have been at the helm of running these organizations for an interval of time rather than a habit or discipline persisting across time in the organizational culture. This preceding statement subtly highlights the need for organizational capabilities in farsightedness that go well beyond some visionary individuals.

I must also reiterate that while it is easy for me to stress on the importance of developing the discipline of 'accurate anticipation' in the management cadre of organizations beyond just a few individuals, it is oftentimes the most intractable of all the organizational initiatives and usually has the lowest degree of widespread success. A significant difference here lies in its substantive dependence on the human instincts developed by managers over time and with experience, which is difficult to substitute with a predefined protocol of scientific tools and processes that are easier to build and to train workforce on their usage.

Psychologist Frances E. Vaughan states: 'Foresight and Intuition is something like a collective wisdom of civilizations, something no software package has so far achieved.'

A pertinent reason for this unique challenge is aptly described by Paul Ormerod in his book.[3] He considers changes in the external environment as a derivative of complex relationships that lead to small but significant changes in the environmental topography. The changes that we see in the external world are an integration of these numerous small but complex phenomena, which is hard to unravel by relatively simple mathematical and

---

[3]Paul Ormerod, *Why Most Things Fail: And How to Avoid It* (London: Faber and Faber, 2005), chapter 2, pp. 17–35.

analytical models that are prolifically used in business forecasting processes. Hence, by nature's machination, most forecasting models tend to be elementary in describing future.

A somewhat 'satisficing' solution to overcome this challenge is to build forecasting processes that gather information about the future from various independent sources, for instance, from scientific and analytical models, as well as subjective and qualitative inputs from individuals with expert knowledge that are based on legacy and experience (and partly bestowed by Providence to a few). These are then churned by heuristics sophisticated enough only for the human brain to apply, which provides the final closer to accurate estimate of the future.

It is easy to perceive the important role of instincts in this process. While some pieces of input information are truly scientific, the final output usually is a strange concoction of both a science and an art of anticipation. This may be the reason why visionary as a trait is associated with only a handful of individuals in the corporate world. Unfortunately, very few organizations have been able to effectively transfer this amorphous competency (should they possess it) across generations of managerial resources as a part of their leadership succession plans.

Timely Transformation (T)

> Even a correct decision is wrong when it was taken too late.
> —Lee Iacocca

'Accurate anticipation' is a necessary condition for a successful organizational transformation (change) process in

a dynamic environment. No significant change is devoid
of aggravation (both physical and psychological) in the
organization. Hence, to replenish and reequip in order to
take on a changing environment, adequate lead time is
required with enough organizational stamina to weather
the challenges of change. Innovation is the building block
for effective change and oftentimes requires an extended
period of time to fructify. A major reason attributable
to many organizational failures is the lack of lead time to
cope with a changing environment (inadequate time to
adapt with newer ideas), perpetuated by the inability
to accurately 'anticipate' the future (see Box 1.2 for what
makes a good innovation climate).

BOX 1.2   Good Innovation Climate: What Is Required?

Besides competency and creativity, fostering innovation
climate requires the following:

1. The desperation to succeed when there are no substi-
   tutes to look up to.
2. The eye to sense a problem and the application to
   resolve it.

To acquire these qualities, organizations may have to
simultaneously overcome complacency and build patience.
Patience from the leadership to allow thorough enquiry
of an innovation opportunity is very necessary to ensure
effective discovery. Most good discoveries take an investment
of lead time and managers of such initiatives must provide
adequate cover and latitude to the innovation process to
work effectively.

(Box 1.2 continued)

(Box 1.2 continued)

At the same time, the organization climate needs to be bereft from complacency associated at times with healthy business performance. It is with the eye to the future that healthy organizations invest in long-duration innovation projects to be able to counter flagging business cycles in a timely fashion with innovation. Needless to say, the best organizations capable of fostering innovation are the ones that encounter good business performance. This is because radical and impactful innovation requires not only significant financial resources but also a longer horizon for it to deliver. Ironically, good performance can many times impair the focus on innovation due to complacency setting in. Management with foresight must do enough to avoid such blemishes. In times of true need for innovative ideas (to tide over a business downturn), organizations may not have the ability to fund innovation in spite of their willingness to do so.

Many organizations in India are struggling to catch up on global standards of innovation. A reason for this sluggishness in Indian economy has been the steady influx of new ideas that have been 'tried and tested' elsewhere. With the domestic economy catching up with global benchmarks and increasing competitiveness in the Indian market that demands better and innovative service at a faster pace, such availability of creative ideas from other markets may dry up soon. Hence, the need for a strong innovative climate to assure a long-term competitive advantage.

Do organizations have a fair chance to survive rapid changes in the environment when anticipating the future is fraught with such high degree of uncertainty?

Coca-Cola in 1985 anticipated that people would want a 'New-Coke'. But actually the consumers did not and within 90 days of the 'new coke fiasco', Coca-Cola back-tracked to its original recipe!

Well, maybe. A key to such survival plan is to build internal processes that can rapidly address changing environmental conditions in a reactive mode. Should an unforeseen circumstance befall the organization, can it respond to the 'calamity' to mould itself in a timely manner?

Just like what Coke did, it knew it had muddled up but bravely it resumed the good old 'coke' without losing further time and market share!

'Quick response' with seamless 'adaptability'[4] along with measures to accumulate resources for a 'rainy day' (Inventory and Portfolio Management and Safety Stock Planning) are some ways that well-managed organizations attempt to mitigate the risks of ineffective 'anticipation'. However, this exposition on 'response time' and 'adaptability' should not shift the focus away from the critical task of building more effective Anticipatory mechanisms in the organization, which is perhaps the most significant catalyst for long-term survival.

Money Matters (M)

If you want quick and effective results you must put the money in.

—Edward Bullard

---

[4]Examples of such managerial interventions are: Organization Design to Build Flexibility, Job Rotation and Retooling.

No one can deny the assistance that financial resources can provide. Any significant transformation in organizations requires enormous stamina and strength to overcome the inertia of incumbency and to cope up with the volatility of a new structure and composition. An important source of such stamina and strength lies in the financial coffers of the organizations. It is hard to manage significant changes in organizations on a lean budget. Most 'emaciated' businesses have limited staying power and almost no latitude to steer change within them. Hence, another reason for transformations to be managed in a timely fashion is to ensure that they are undertaken when the organization has enough financial strength to enable the acquisition of the right resources for the future. Many timely transformations with an eye on future opportunities are undertaken when the organization is cash-rich and still raking money by mining its current opportunities. The key is to avoid the 'complacency trap' that financial strength and strong current performance create by looking beyond the current euphoria and be able to 'coldly' assess the competency requirements for the future.

That summarizes the discipline of the 'ATM'. It is worth reiterating that the fuel to the successful deployment of this discipline lies largely in the effectiveness of first component (anticipation). If we were to trace back to the success stories of many respected corporate leaders of India and the world that we have discussed in various business settings, it is most likely that people pay tribute to their 'farsightedness' and 'vision beyond the immediate'.

It is not difficult to perceive why. Unfortunately, there are fewer instances of business success that transcend beyond the tenure of a specific individual or a group of individuals.

I must highlight the similarity of this construct to the age-old strategic framework proposed by the Boston Consulting Group (BCG matrix). Most management graduates will be familiar with this construct. While the BCG framework is a useful methodology to evaluate the overall health of the business portfolio of any organization, the ATM utilizes its core output (the classification of business units on the basis of future potential) to guide smart managers to affect appropriate investments in the future in a timely fashion (Figure 1.1).

FIGURE 1.1   The 'ATM' Framework for Managing Business

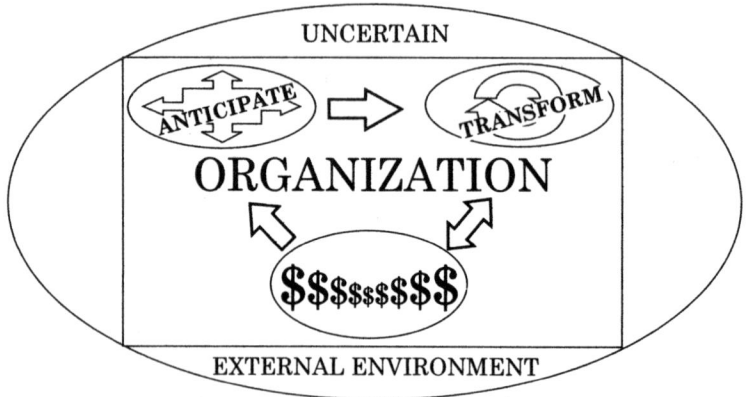

It is difficult to identify, an organization in recent history has managed this discipline of the 'ATM' very well over the long run. Probably many profit-making organizations in the long run have successfully developed this discipline when compared to their competitors, but whether they have done it well enough is hard to tell. There have also been cases of successful and reputable organizations ending up being less so over the years primarily for not staying in tune with changing environment—the Big Three Auto Companies in the United States should largely fall in this category. At the same time, many respected and long-lasting organizations in very dynamic environments such as telecom (e.g., Ericsson and Huawei), information technology and outsourcing[5] e.g., Genpact and Infosys) and high end technology (Intel and IBM) have battled with appropriate and timely transformations to cope with changes in the external environment. Only time can deliver the verdict on their ability to transition appropriately like they have done in the past. What is a fact is that many of these organizations have indeed transformed their competency 'make up' to address changes in external stakeholder requirements. Intel[6] is far more 'front-office' oriented compared to a largely 'Technology and R&D' focused organization that it was more than 25 years ago. Similarly, IBM is significantly more 'service-driven' compared to its original focus on 'products'.

---

[5]Arindam Banerjee and Scott A. Williams, 'International Service Outsourcing: Using Offshore Analytics to Identify Determinants of Value-added Outsourcing', *Strategic Outsourcing: An International Journal* 2, (1, 2009): 68–79.

[6]'Intel Corporation—Leveraging Capabilities for Strategic Renewal', HBS Publishing Division Case 9-394-141, March 1994.

The fact of the matter is that for every cited case of a successful organization in transition, there are many cases of failures, mostly unknown and unheralded. Failure is unfortunately a part of organizations' life and 'age tells on them all'.[7] Even organizations that have been successful over a period of time have eventually disappeared. What perhaps distinguishes between long-lasting organizations and others which have not been so may well be the former group's better adoption of the discipline of 'ATM' in creating 'value' to their customers on an ongoing basis.

NET-OF-NET, WHAT ARE WE TALKING ABOUT?

The net of all this is that there are no antidotes for immortality of business organizations. As competitiveness increases, the probability of a typical organization to survive longer actually reduces. And while increasing competitiveness is generally good for the markets, industry and consumers as a whole, it does make it harder for individual organizations to stay profitable in the long run, unless of course they remain at the forefront of competitiveness continuously. It is perhaps appropriate to say that, when you have scaled the highest mountain, there is no time to elate. The next challenge of staying on top for long is as difficult, if not more. The executives of the top-performing firms never get time to celebrate

---

[7]Alfred Marshall, *Principles of Economics* (London: Macmillan, 1890).

their achievements. There is no time for complacency, lest they unwittingly let go of their premier positions in business. In the following three chapters, I will delve into the core acumen that successful business organizations need to build—'The Power of Anticipation' and the 'Ability of Timely Reaction' and the need for critical resources including money (Money Matters). Fundamentally, these are the three engines that power business organizations and are the motivations behind most management theory and practice.

Two

THE POWER OF ANTICIPATION

THE 'CURRY' INGREDIENTS

May you live in interesting times.

—Chinese curse

Most entrepreneurs would love to usurp the skills of anticipation. There are no rewards for guessing the obvious. If we could anticipate the future perfectly, we could all plan to confront the future without any qualms of facing the unknown and unexpected. On a lighter vein, while it would be great to have control over the future, it would also make our lives a lot more boring. The fact is that the unanticipated element of the future is what makes our lives interesting.

> I have always been delighted at the prospect of a new day, a fresh try, one more start, with perhaps a bit of magic waiting somewhere behind the morning.
>
> —Joseph Priestley

But try telling that to the entrepreneur who has wagered his monetary investment in a risky venture called the enterprise. For him, a perfectly unanticipated future is like gambling his money—you win sometimes and you lose as well with equal frequency.

Most of the time, investor wisdom would try to do better than the probability of success associated with a lottery. This would mean that a businessman's goal would be to reduce the probability of adversity (or anticipate the same with close to perfection) to ensure that he makes judicious choices with regards to wagering his money invested in enterprise.

To stretch the argument to the extreme, entrepreneurs would love to develop an anticipatory mechanism that forecasts the future with perfection, hoping that it would end all speculations about the future and provide assured and known returns on their investments. Additionally, that would be perfect information for optimal planning with respect to investment decisions for the future.

Thankfully, no such system exists other than in very staid and extremely stagnant business environments (if such environments occur). Profit-making embodies a certain amount of risk taking, which is intrinsically linked with our inability to foretell for sure. Additionally, as described earlier, this inability to perfect the 'art' of foretelling generates employment for hundreds of management graduates in today's business environment, who, instigated by the challenge placed by their employers (entrepreneurs), invest their time and energy in building 'better' anticipatory mechanisms than what exists today, in the hope that prospective planning would be easier to do. To the extent the future still holds surprises, management remains alert to react wisely and adjust initiatives as the situation demands in a timely manner, for the goodness of the organization and the investor (profit making in most cases).

> Business, more than any other occupation, is a continual dealing with the future; it is a continual calculation, an instinctive exercise in foresight.
>
> —Henry Luce

Also, my own observations on the way enterprises are managed led me to conclude that anticipation, or the lack of it, is a core reason for the need for formal principles of enterprise management.

In my numerous interactions with people in enterprise, I have often been asked to help organizations to set up effective planning processes for the future. The most important elements to the client in these engagements have been issues about foresight usually articulated as 'what is the future and where do we see us in the future?' Evidently, if there is a perfect clarity on this dimension, planning would be lot less complex.

For reasons, and to some extent, beyond my individual competence, many of my 'futuristic planning' engagements with business enterprises have not met the kind of expectations set by my clients. Apart from the impossible challenge of building a perfect anticipatory mechanism, it is also unreasonable for managers to expect turnkey solutions to such complex problems from outside advisors and consultants.

The true power of anticipation is developed over time and is usually a strange concoction of many processes and methodologies that are deeply entrenched in extremely different philosophies of 'logic', namely scientific as well as pseudo-scientific, bordering on non-rational sensibilities. These two radically opposite approaches provide the holistic backdrop, necessary for a well-rounded view of the unknown. They may include, among other things, (a) scientific processes of systematic pattern recognition from historical and current market data, (b) observing independent trends in other domains that overtly need not have any direct impact on the current enterprise, (c) assessing hunches and feelings captured by human senses through deep-rooted connect with the realities of the environment (something science can never systematically defend), (d) disciplining employees at the enterprise-wide level to collate information from all these various sources in order to create multiple scenarios of the future, and (e) taking a vote amongst the experts and visionaries on which scenarios best depict the likely development in the future. Sometimes, the final stage of forecasting revolves around employing instincts developed over time, which no scientific and rational process can match, in helping you deliver the same or even enhanced level of confidence and comfort.

> A moment's insight is sometimes worth a life's experience.
> —Oliver Wendell Holmes

Imminently, a disciplined approach of meticulously incorporating a comprehensive view of the future developed through various lenses of analysis requires investment in time and patience. A healthy organizational culture, which continuously and painstakingly collects signals from the environment and pieces them together to construct the 'image' of the future, is needed to be built. Historically, some acclaimed entrepreneurs have exhibited better than average instincts at envisioning the future and therefore their track records in business have been notable. Consider the case of Richard Branson's decision to enter the airline business back in 1984. He states, 'It was a move which in pure economic terms everybody thought was mad, including my closest friends but it was something which I felt we could bring something to that others were not bringing.' So Branson followed his instinct, and succeeded in delivering what he envisioned in an entirely new industry.

On the other hand, many others have been unsuccessful in emulating the same traits and have fallen to the wayside. Once a world leader in photographic equipment, Eastman Kodak overlooked the digital revolution even when its smaller competitors were turning that way; result—the film camera that gave us the first click of our lives shall now become a memory in itself. Eastman Kodak, established in 1892, a leader till the 1980s, filed for bankruptcy in 2012 and completely exited the business of cameras.

From the given examples, I would think that for every recorded instance of a successful enterprise that has anticipated environmental changes quite well and reacted appropriately, there may be thousands of unrecorded failures of organizations and their leaders not having been successful in adhering to the same principles.

Unfortunately, as stated elsewhere, the power of anticipation is one that is difficult to acquire. Formal education can only teach distinct methodologies (statistical techniques, experimentation, Delphi techniques) that form the building blocks for any forecasting/anticipation process. However, what is unclear is the correct choice of methods to be used for a specific context to drive the process of finding convergence across information available from various methods employed. Although there are some very broad correlations between utility of certain family of methods with the dynamics of the business environment, on the whole, the process development remains an art that requires to be mastered with experience. Conclusively quoting the legendry Andrew Lang, 'An unsophisticated forecaster uses statistics as a drunken man uses lampposts—for support rather than for illumination.'

For the sake of completeness, I shall describe some of the methods used for creating processes helpful for anticipating the future.

1. *Historical data analysis:*

> In the business world, the rear-view mirror is always clearer than the windshield.
>
> —Warren Buffet

History provides great insights about what happened and why it happened and also sometimes the possibility of it happening again in the future. When systematic and quantifiable data are available, there is a tendency to overemphasize the importance of such analysis, mainly due to the ease of applying multiple scientific tools to process data and elegantly extract inferences. The only fear is that elegance may at times outweigh the true value of the insight from history, more so when the future is dynamic and therefore may not mirror the past.

2. *Market experiments:* Oftentimes when history is unhelpful in providing leads into the future, the best way to find hard evidence of the future is to simply 'test the water' in a cautious manner and extrapolate the findings based on the test for the future. Radically new propositions/initiatives when have no close precedence are often subject to methods such as these to provide assistance in prediction.

Stuart Crainer in his book, *The 75 Greatest Management Decisions Ever Made,* talks about how Walmart tested the waters before its full-fledged entrance into the Grocery Retail Industry:

> Put your toes in water, not your legs: Wal Mart experimented and tried the Hypermarket format out in a limited number of locations. The stores were enormous (220,000 square feet), complex, costly and made small profits, but they were important sources of learning. Most important the company acted on what it learned from them.

Today, Walmart has more than 8,500 stores around the world. Testing the waters and employing the learning can really help.

3. *Expert advice of the 'fortune teller':* Obviously the icing to all methodologies is provided by the human brain, which has the flexibility of churning information of a scale, no computing architecture can match. Besides, the expert advice of someone who is grounded in the environment and has significant exposure to the vagaries of it, and hopefully has genetically pronounced instincts, can really provide insights that can calibrate the baseline predictions

made by more consistent but 'constrained' methodologies described earlier. Recorded literature terms these semi-structured processes as Delphi Techniques, used extensively in more dynamic business environments.

THREE PREREQUISITES FOR BUILDING GOOD PROCESS OF ANTICIPATION

If a man will begin with certainties he shall end in doubts; but if he will be content to begin with doubts he shall end in certainties.

—Francis Bacon

There are subtle variations of the discussed broad methodologies followed in building processes for anticipation. The important point to be remembered is that to build good anticipatory mechanisms, organizations would require the following:

1. *Discipline of considering multiple sources of information that project the future:* This discipline cannot be developed in a short while and hence patience to invest and the flexibility to have a margin of error are very necessary. Additionally, this discipline needs to be developed across a large section of the organization and not just amongst the specialist forecasters.

2. *Projecting the future with the help of multiple methods and independent sources of information:* Projecting the unknown future requires adequate confidence in the emerging scenarios. A reliable

method to build consistency is to evaluate the future projection through multiple independent avenues and see if the projections converge. Either way, this approach provides evidence about the strength of the futuristic projections. A caution is justified at this stage. Analyzing multiple independent sources of information is never simplistic and recognizing patterns across them can be tricky and time-consuming, to say the least.

3. *Evolving a specialist forecasting function with multiple expertise:* While this may sound ordinary, it requires an emphatic reiteration. Many organizations, in my opinion, fail to acknowledge the need for multiple expertise to develop the forecasting function; partly because, the planning initiative in organizations is rarely associated directly with the revenue earning of the organization and hence it is perpetually pressured to question its existence. The reality of maintaining healthy bottom line in the short run has relegated most planning functions to line managers, who may usually have a myopic view of the business, given their preoccupation with more immediate requirements of business.

CONCLUSION

In conclusion, let me iterate the difficulty of creating a successful forecasting process that provides close to perfect anticipation and serves as a critical input to the planning function of organizations. In most business environments, subjected to dynamic movements, forecasting as a function remains very ineffective for various reasons. Creation of effective forecasting processes requires investments that are significant and their fructification occurs only over a longer horizon. Most managers, preoccupied in immediate business performances, may find it challenging to pay too much attention to this very important long-term investment in business processes. Edgar R. Fiedler in 'The Three Rs of Economic Forecasting—Irrational, Irrelevant and Irreverent' simply puts this idea as 'If you have to forecast, forecast often'.

Three

WHEN YOU CAN'T ANTICIPATE WELL, YOU MUST REACT ON TIME

ANOTHER CURRY INGREDIENT

'No, no!' said the Queen. 'Sentence first—verdict afterwards.'

—Lewis Carroll

Lack of effective anticipatory mechanisms in most organizations is the cause for building management processes that react well to changing environment. It is easy to perceive the dichotomy—proaction is strategically very portent, but if proactive measures are ineffective due to faulty prediction, practitioners are well advised to invest significantly in resource mobilization to ensure timely and deft reactive measures as the future unfolds.

Theoretically, it is better to adopt proactive strategies, if possible, since the cost of reaction is never anywhere close to being insignificant. However, as described earlier, most forecasting systems are at best half-baked (with lots of leakages) and hence relying on satisfactory reactive processes serves as a good and necessary complement for successful business performance in the long run.

A company needs to have good business reflexes, to be able to marshal its forces in a crisis or in response to any unplanned event.

—Bill Gates

WHAT ARE INVESTMENTS FOR EFFECTIVE REACTION?

I will classify reactive investments broadly into two buckets: *(a)* investment in versatility and *(b)* investment in creating buffers ('buying' insurance).

Investment in Versatility

The person who figures out how to harness the collective genius of his or her organization is going to blow the competition away.

—Walter Wriston

Who can deny the value of versatility especially if such talent can be deployed without delay? Unfortunately, such idealistic processes are rare, if at all. To give an example of versatility, HR departments across organizations would ideally like to identify and retain talent that exhibits multi-faceted skills that are relevant for the organization at different points in time. Cross-training initiatives are usually encouraged in organizations to build a semblance of versatility among employees to take on jobs other than their own specializations, if the need arises. In principle, the value of any employee increases with the increasing demand for the skills that she provides. Additionally, if she has capability to 'effortlessly' transition to newer skills as the requirement changes, her valuation is upped even further. Needless to say, employee compensations are intrinsically linked to the perceived value they provide in creating business output, in a perfectly market-driven economy.

Investment decisions on assets usually require a review of the flexibility of utilization of the same. Assets such as plant and machinery are considered more valuable, if they can be utilized flexibly for creating outputs in line with changing requirements of the market. I was once informed by a budding entrepreneur in the growing private sector for professional education during a meeting at his office that he intended to invest heavily in land and infrastructure; he planned to invest minimally in faculty, only to the extent that would be required to satisfy the minimum standards set by the relevant state academic regulatory board. Faculty, according to him, was not a flexible resource, unlike infrastructure. A professor of dentistry was useful only in a dental school and nowhere else. On the other hand, with changing demand for various professional education programmes (business studies, medicine, dentistry, etc.), he could easily 'recycle' his infrastructure to offer different professional educational programmes as per market demand. For example, the classrooms could be refurbished with relative ease for any type of professional training requirements. With regards to faculty, he noted that his operating model was compatible with sourcing largely part-time and contractual faculty who required little upfront investment and were more easily replaceable with changing demand. Notwithstanding the scant regard for ethical issues portrayed in this example, I cannot deny the heightened sense of commercial acumen that the entrepreneur was portraying that day while describing his forays in the recently opened social entrepreneurship sector in the country.

'Outsourcing' is another trend that builds versatility in organizations. Assuming that outsourced vendors perform reliably and a willing to scale up or scale down services with changing requirements almost seamlessly, the phenomenon is a great example of how organizations in the competitive world have managed to keep their inflexible commitments under check to increase high returns. The downside is that reliable vendors who match up in performance to such exacting standards are few and usually come with a higher price tag, which invariably has an adverse impact on the output cost. Be that as it may, such practices have increased the manager's control over costs and have helped in better alignment of the upfront investment to output requirements.

Be Cautious to Address a Contingency

> Make sure that any big bet that the company makes is above the waterline and that the company will not sink as a result of the bet failing.
> —Jim Collins in *How the Mighty Fall*

This principle cannot be simpler than what is stated—'to save for a rainy day'. We all do that in our personal lives. When times are good, we save a bit for the day when an adversity may strike. Many operating principles learnt at business schools have their genesis from this simple motivation. The idea is to set aside some proportion for addressing the unknown change that may take up. It can also be stated as 'buying an insurance' against eventualities.

When the business environment looks optimistic, our planning incorporates a buffer (redundancy) to deal with the unpredictable optimism. We would not like to miss out on the additional opportunity that may come due to a positive unpredictability. Similarly, when there is a general pessimism about the future business environment, caution sets in and there is a penchant to downsize the plan below the best expected to account for the eventuality. In formal management parlance, this behaviour is usually termed as risk averseness. Building redundancies, safety stock to address an additional windfall, and so on, are some of the ways business managers use to address unpredictability of the future in case there is a high cost associated with missing the opportunity.

On the other hand, pessimism would tilt the planning southward of the expected futuristic prediction in line with the risk averseness behaviour of the manager. In this case, 'safe' planning practice to counter an adverse condition would require scaling down output below the expectation to account for the high cost of accumulation due to the market not demanding enough.

The concept of building adequate contingency measures based on futuristic projections is no different from the dilemma that individuals face while making decisions related to managing personal wealth. Optimism regarding the future, supported by a somewhat generous dose of 'risk taking' characteristics, can influence personal investments into riskier portfolio of stocks and equities for an expected high yield in the long run. On the contrary, pessimism about the future can swing decisions to the other end of the spectrum wherein investors are contented with assured but low returns in bonds and bank deposits.

FUTURISTIC PLANNING IN UNCERTAINTY: THE 'ANOMALY' CALLED EXPECTATION

> Only one thing is certain—that is, nothing is certain. If this statement is true, it is also false.
>
> —Ancient Paradox

Walking the thin line as described above, 'optimal' business paradigms are usually developed based on the central tendency of a stochastic future projection. A mean or expectation is the popular index of a central tendency used to compute (deduce) the optimal decision output. However, here lies a fundamental disconnect between a central tendency-based decision algorithm and the reality. The principle of expectation (mean) assumes that if the future were to unfold an infinite number of times, the mean (expected) value would be the 'middle value' of the future performance across these infinite iterations.

In reality, businesses and their managers do not have the opportunity to do course correction based on infinite trials. On the contrary, they get only one chance to take decisions before the environment of the future unfolds to show its true self. Hence, banking on an expected value of the future (the central tendency of a probability distribution) may not always appeal to them. Informed choices are still based on imperfect information about the future and hence managers are forced to adjust decisions from the central tendency to account for what they perceive as an optimistic/pessimistic trend for the future. These adjustments are made based on more qualitative view of the future, the resilience of the organization to weather an adverse condition and the risk appetite of the decision-makers.

Chris Corrigan, who inspired the series *Bastard Boys* and was amidst the infamous waterfront dispute that shook Australia in 1998, reflected upon the given enigma as:

> I think the most important CEO task is defining the course that the business will take over the next five or so years. You have to have the ability to see what the business environment might be like a long way out, not just over the coming months. You need to be able to both set a broad direction, and also to take particular decisions along the way that make that broad direction unfold correctly.

Having stated the divergence of reality from theory, I must re-emphasize the value of core theoretical underpinnings for decision-makers to calibrate their decisions wisely. Expected values based on probability distribution of future scenarios serve as a strong and reliable basis for decision-makers to evaluate their decisions and recalibrate, taking account of additional constraints imposed by their context and their individual personality traits. Rational paradigms provide a good foundation for decision-making, although good decisions also need to satisfy the sufficiency conditions based on contextual imperatives.

Suffice to say that rationality has its limitations, especially when decisions have to be made that affect human kind. Our business organizations work for, with and are comprised of human beings—who need not necessarily (almost never) behave rationally. Hence, it is natural to question the need for rationality driving many of management theory, which appears rather simplistic in a more complex setting like a societal environment. Nevertheless, it still forms a strong foundation to identify consistent output. The trained human brain should be receptive to such rationality, and at the same time, be amenable to make modifications as the specific context demands.

Four

SOME CRUCIAL INPUTS FOR RUNNING THE ORGANIZATION

THE 'CURRY' CONDIMENTS

Having looked at the mechanics of running an organization and its governance from a 'high plane', it will be prudent to focus for a bit on the inputs required for keeping the organizational machinery running smoothly. The fundamental inputs that no one can ignore are money, labour and information, in varying proportions depending on the business domain. All are very critical for management purpose. Money that buys all the resources needed for running the enterprise, labour that provides the 'horse power' to keep the organization running and information that provides appropriate guidance on how to deploy money and labour wisely. In Chapter 1, we described an effective organization as one that utilizes its eternally constrained financial resources by effectively deploying its human resources to get the maximum 'bang for the buck' using the available information resources wisely. To be able to do so, there are a few governing principles and issues to be aware of, which are recounted here.

FINANCIAL RESOURCE

I gave him an unlimited budget and he exceeded it.
—Edward Bennett Williams

The inception of an enterprise and its subsequent operation requires money in the form of capital, and/or debt and benevolent grants. Capital and debt are the major forms of money supply and require deft handling and allocation to ensure that the entrepreneur is careful about managing the final return to adequately compensate his lot for the risk he takes for running the enterprises. There are of course certain advantages and disadvantage of both forms of funding, which, to an average business school graduate, should be obvious. Debt serves as a simple straightforward form of fund availability at the expense of a fixed and committed price (interest) over a pre-determined tenure, irrespective of the final financial condition of the enterprise. For all practical purposes, a debt investor does not assume any risk of losing funds (unless in the case of a bankruptcy of the debtor), but has a fixed income stream. Financially solvent enterprises do not see this fund source as a problem, since their ability to repay the fixed fee and the principal sum at the end of the tenure is usually routine and trivial. However, organizations operating in environments with fluctuating fortunes oftentimes have to worry about the debt burden that they carry due to the fixed and time-bound liability of interest.

To avoid this large debt burden, especially in a risky environment or, in instances where returns may fructify over a longer term, capital infusion is often a good option. Capital absorbs much of the time-bound risk of repayment as there are no fixed time liabilities of pay-back of capital infused or, income payment for the same. Therefore, from a 'commitment to a return' stand point, it carries the minimum risk. At the same time, larger capital infusion into the organization will naturally dilute the rate of return for a constant absolute income obtained. For instance, if the founder of a start-up injects an initial capital of ₹1,000 in the firm, he gets to control of the earnings after taxes and interest (net income). However, if he injects further capital to the order of ₹2,000 from an external entity, he would theoretically have to divide the Net Income generated in the ratio of the injected capital by various entities. Additionally, if the capital infusion comes from several sources, the ownership of the enter-prise gets diluted with many entities claiming a share of the organization. Management control can be challenging in this case with several entities vying to leverage their ownership rights to steer the organization in their desired trajectory. Healthy governance protocol is required to ensure seamless operations of such organization accounting for diverse expectations of a large ownership base.

Ideally, it would be great for the entrepreneur to finance his enterprise by funding the entire amount through his own capital. The advantage being that neither is he overburdened by the fixed limited time liability of repayment of the debt with interest, nor does he have to part with the control of his organization or share the income generated by the enterprise with other part owners of the organization. Normally, such an idealistic situation rarely holds beyond a certain scale of operation. An individual investor is typically constrained by his ability to infuse large amounts of capital required for rapid growth, and external sources of funding become a necessity, along with their associated complexities.

HUMAN RESOURCE

> People are definitely a company's greatest asset. It doesn't make any difference whether the product is cars or cosmetics. A company is only as good as the people it keeps.
>
> —Mary Kay Ash

The science of fund management is somewhat moderated by the 'art' of managing people and their psyche. A rather difficult and challenging task for most organization, as mentioned before, the unpredictability of the business environment is driven to a large extent by the various roles that human beings assume in the business environment.

A significant aberration that needs to be managed is the unpredictability of the employee, a necessary but difficult task. Unfortunately, a large bit of this domain remains more perceptive than can be taught in a classroom. A good reason perhaps, for it not being a popular area of study at many business schools.

While I do not claim any expertise in this very important area of management knowledge, I would still want to add a few words of advice from my own experience of managing people. People management requires capable leadership, which enables organization to achieve their true potential in the long run. Theoretically, it would mean to expect the optimum amount of output from each employee given his/her potential and to compensate him/her fairly (at market clearing rates). Additionally, good leaders command respect from the rank and file, not because of the position that they assume, but for the quality of the individual. Good leadership qualities include empathy and respect for people, understanding of the complexity of tasks that are delegated, the ability to envision the objective and to build a reasonable amount of consensus among the employees to work towards achieving the same, and the ability to groom subordinates to succeed them in their role as leaders in the future. Strong leaders realize that their tenure of leadership is finite and for organizations to run successfully, they require successors that match up to them or exhibit even stronger qualities than themselves. A notable example of such succession planning was that of Roberto Goizueta, the legendary chairman of Coca-Cola in the eighties and nineties. Goizueta identified his probable successor early in his tenure as CEO of Coke and groomed him for over 14 years, till his somewhat unexpected death in 1997. He realized early that succession could be an issue overnight and he made sure that the company he loved was ready. Douglas Ivester was ready to be anointed as Goizueta's successor. In fact, succession planning under Goizueta went beyond his immediate reports. Over his tenure, Goizueta ensured that a dozen young talented executives were groomed under Ivester for building the management prowess at Coke for the future.[1] *The Economist*[2] commented: 'Roberto Goizueta will be deeply mourned at Coca-Cola, but he may not be missed. Strangely enough,

---

[1]*Businessweek*, 'Commentary: What Other CEOs Can Learn from Goizueta', 3 November 1997.

[2]*The Economist*, 25 October 1997.

that would be the greatest compliment a departed chief executive could receive ....'

It is noteworthy that Ivester retired from Coke within two years of his appointment as CEO and chairman after being at the helm of some indifferent business performance of the company. While Goizueta's long-lasting contribution to his company remains intact, in retrospect, industry watchers have commented that although Goizueta's succession planning process was right, the choice of his successor was not. In effect, Ivester was a perfect complement to Goizueta, but could not fill the void created by his departure.

In my opinion, good organizations can continue to perform well when backed by strong financial strength. But, they necessarily require dedicated and competent human workforce to drive the performance. I could part with the former (financial prowess) to some extent, but I would never compromise on good people. Grooming good human resources involves making right choices early and investing in time to develop them. Unfortunately, losing them can happen almost instantaneously due to attrition and can strip organizations of their best resources almost overnight. Careful investment and maintenance of the people asset in organizations is an enormous challenge for all organizations. To close, the much talked Level 5 Leadership concept by Jim Collins talks about this in an interesting way, 'First Who, Then What: Those who build great organizations make sure they have the right people on the bus, the wrong people off the bus, and the right people in the key seats before they figure out where to drive the bus.'

INFORMATION RESOURCE

> Bringing together the right information with the right people
> will dramatically improve a company's ability to develop and
> act on strategic business opportunities.
>
> —Bill Gates

This intangible resource is proving to be the dealmaker (or breaker) in the current era. Information resources when available contribute significantly to the health of business, provided management is equipped to use them effectively. More often than not, practitioners rue the non-availability of proper data that incapacitates them from taking a more comprehensive review of a business problem resolution (see Figure 4.1).

Non-availability of critical information resources in organization can act like 'slow and oblivious poison', especially when management is ignorant about the virtues of the same. Historically, most successful organizations have managed their fortunes due to the business acumen of a 'few good men' at the helm, who have acquired appropriate nuggets of market wisdom and applied them effectively to take the right decisions. It will be foolhardy to discount the value of the 'few good men' at the helm of many businesses and their collective business acumen. For a significant time period of documented business history in India, competitive advantage has been sustained by passing on 'trade secrets' to the next generation in major family-run businesses. Accumulated wisdom in the 'closed' family circle was and, still is, considered critical to maintain the primacy of the business in many such

FIGURE 4.1 Strategic Marketing Decision-Making Process

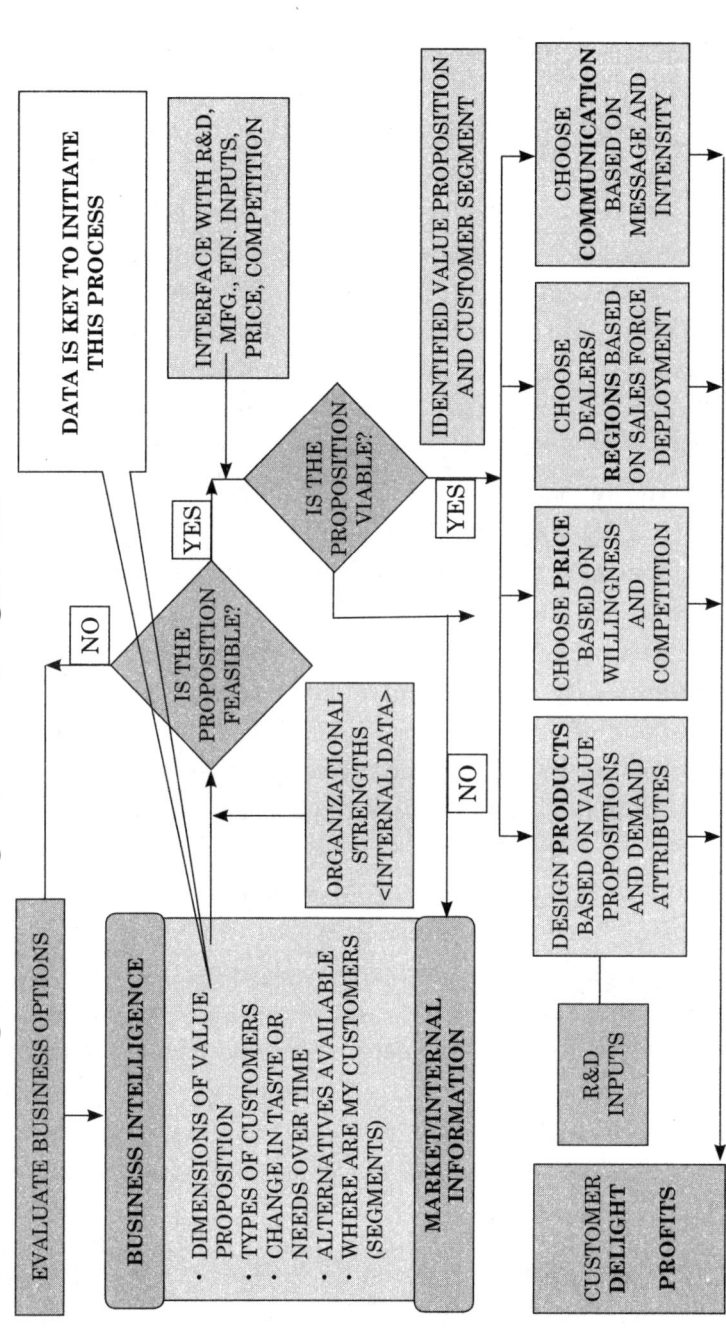

Source: Author's own.

enterprises. Collectivism,[3] as against individual pursuits based on rationality, meant following traditional rules and practices that had been steadfastly abided by over years and considered as closely guarded secrets. Not too long ago, recruitment of senior management professionals in family-led businesses was highly influenced by community and territorial alignments. For instance, I was once told that the recruitment of a certain Chief Finance Officer (CFO) in a family-owned organization was largely influenced by the fact that the particular individual belonged to a village (and owned a significant piece of land) in the vicinity of the ancestral place of the business family. That was considered a relatively important piece of information to swing the decision in his favour, compared to his grasp of financial acumen. In such business environments, acquired scientific acumen by 'better' and more formally educated members of the business community is oftentimes looked upon with suspicion, and investments in organizational assets that may enhance decision-making capabilities beyond the 'select few' are summarily discouraged. Therefore, the lament about 'lack of data' in organizations can be misleading. In reality, it can also be an effective ruse to avoid investing in internal capabilities that are perceived to improve business acumen of the 'rank and file', not necessarily considered a worthwhile initiative to sustain a competitive advantage.

However, with increasing competition and the consequent need for higher precision in decision-making, relying solely on intuition or individual acumen can be

---

[3] Harry Traindis, *Individualism and Collectivism* (Boulder, Colorado: Westview Press, 1995); Sheena Iyengar, *The Art of Choosing* (United Kingdom: Little, Brown, 2010).

increasingly ineffective. This issue has been dealt with in some detail in a previous section; however, suffice to say, like human resources, investment in this arena takes much longer to fructify and hence is a true game changer for businesses that have the foresight to invest early.

In conclusion, it must be highlighted that judicious[4] deployment of organizational resources namely, finance, human power and information is the key to reaping maximum returns in the long run. These important ingredients by themselves do not build strong organizations. Organizational leaders still require the business acumen expostulated in earlier sections as a good recipe to mix the ingredients in the right proportion to create effective business outcomes.

Of these resources, deployment of finances is perceptibly easier, but has much riskier consequences. Being an input into almost every type of business investment, the extent to which it is smartly deployed determines the health of the organization in the long run.

---

[4]As described in Chapter 1.

Five

ANALYSIS, THE GROUNDWORK
FOR GOOD DECISION-MAKING

THE CULINARY INFRASTRUCTURE

> Conducting data analysis is like drinking a fine wine. It is
> important to swirl and sniff the wine, to unpack the complex
> bouquet and to appreciate the experience. Gulping the wine
> doesn't work.
>
> —Daniel B. Wright

I had set out to write this manuscript with the hope to
provide a usable framework for the business acumen that
we teach at management schools and practice in parts
in industry. If there is one thing that B-school educated
graduates take pride in, it is their ability to analyze and
reanalyze issues threadbare. And most notably, it is the
one thing that participants in management training programmes can be taught to an extent. What is left to their
intrinsic talent, in good faith, is their ability to sense
when analysis has to end and decisions have to be taken,
never mind how imperfect the analytical output may be
to provide the exact answer to their business quandary.

By now, it must be clear to the reader that rarely
in management decision-making, analysis can provide

a clear and comprehensively defensible option for decision. As has been stated earlier, that is precisely why we need well-heeled human interfaces to finally take the decision-making 'leap' after due consideration of options. The significant role of analysis is less to do with providing a solution. It is to showcase well-considered options by eliminating many others that analysis may prove to be irrelevant or unworthy of further consideration.

In many instances, the strategic role of analysis in decision-making is of reducing options to a smaller set, rather than identifying 'the option'. In the process, it reduces the probability of taking wrong decisions, but very rarely points out the 'best option'. Hence, the genesis of the term 'judgemental leap'. There comes a time when the manager sets aside analysis and takes the 'leap of faith'. Putting in the right perspective, analysis is a good discipline to ensure 'due diligence', necessary to be sure that the review process is able to pick the better alternatives consistently and without any gross aberrations.

But the more difficult question for managers to address is: 'When to stop analyzing further?' Again, rationality will proclaim that the stopping criterion is determined when the incremental worth of further analysis is nil. But the knack to sense at a point in time that it may not be worthwhile to 'analyze further' is something that managers pick up with experience. Sometimes, it is also dependent on the immediacy of the decision-making. As the legendry John Tuke advised, 'An approximate answer to the right problem is worth a good deal more than an exact answer to an approximate problem.' I suspect a trained business school graduate ends up spending more time on analysis and, as her career progresses, the time spent in pondering over information tends to reduce significantly for many valid reasons as stated here.

THE INPUTS FOR SUPERIOR ANALYSIS

Let me now turn the focus on the building blocks of business analysis needed for supporting decision-making. In terms of ingredients, it requires information (data), an analytical processor (brain) and an implication generator (so what). Among the three, 'Data' is usually the most important and difficult asset to invest for creating a good analytical system in organization.

Formal business education has done a reasonably good job of training graduates in analytical processes and the implications. However, the criticism from practice is that frequently such training is not useful because of the lack of data that feeds such an exercise. Given such constraints, it is presumed that analysis can be substituted by 'gut feel' and instincts developed under the tutelage of experienced managers. While the claim has much credibility, there can be some significant divergence to such philosophy. First, experience need not be a substitute for more formal analytics, but can be a very healthy and appropriate complement. Second, and more importantly, the reliance of individual-based 'gut feel' can be dangerous for the organization given that it creates too much reliance on the capabilities of a few individuals. In the book *Closing the Execution Gap: How Great Leaders and Their Companies Get Results*, Richard Lepsinger stresses that involving the right people in the right decisions is one of the most defining steps to bridge the 'execution gaps' in organizations. He says:

> Involving employees in decision-making is controversial. Some leaders view it as a sign of weakness while others fear giving up control. In reality, though, the world is too complex for any leader to go it alone. To make good decisions, you must seek out the perspectives of a wide range of people.

Developing processes that progressively rely less on specific individuals is a very good aspiration for sustaining long-lasting organizational health. This is usually a safer bet to ensure that organization continues to thrive in spite of the (non)availability of some specific individuals. For individual tenures may be short lived, the organization is supposed to maintain good health for long and attain 'immortality'.

Third, externally sourced information-based analysis is normally a good method to avoid making too many subjective and potentially rash decisions. Further, it makes the decision-making process more transparent and inclusive across management cadre, which usually helps improve the psychological health of the work environment.

But, the reality in Indian business environment is that the availability of structured information for decision-making is normally difficult to access and in situations where it is accessible is not in a form that lends itself to rigorous analysis. While there is still a surfeit of information available for tactical level decision-making, for more strategic decisions, the information availability reduces dramatically. No wonder, our tools to fight the these, like enterprise resource planning (ERP) systems, in spite of their theoretical appeal have done precious little to improve decision support through rigorous analytical processing because of the non-availability of strategically important data.

Some business domains have fared better in data capture than others, namely financial services, organized retailing, hospitality and similar service sector industries, to name a few. Their advantage is driven by the fact that the core functioning of these businesses depends on the continuous generation and update of customer data and other business databases and hence 'data creation' is embedded in the functioning of these businesses.

Nevertheless, non-availability of data, in the form, useful for analysis cannot be a credible excuse for not building more rigorous decision support systems in India, especially with formidable global competition creeping into our business environment. With greater intensity of competition, the margin to accommodate erroneous decisions reduces drastically. Precision and accuracy become necessary for survival of the business and hence the need for fact-based rigorous analysis support to decision-making.

It has taken long for evolved markets to create and share industry data that are used by all participating organizations and, that provide access to their own information to the industry data. It requires mutual respect, cooperation and trust to ensure that the data are comprehensive and useful to all participants. At the same time, sensitive information is camouflaged to protect individual organization's interest. It has also required the emergence of competent industry experts to plan, devise, collate and organize the data of the years to make them worthy for analysis and decision-making. Today, the competitiveness across organizations has evolved from 'who has the data' to 'who can process it wisely' and wagers the right bets about the future environment. This investment in time and energy is required and will eventually build up in evolving markets like India as well, since there are no conceivable short cuts possible to attain the same. In this context, I refer the reader to a paper that was published by the author (Appendix) over a decade ago, when the retail revolution in India was still in its nascent stage. The paper emphasizes the need to leverage the then newly created retail transaction data compiled by large retailers to resolve some very critical retail planning issues. With the passage of time, some progress has been made in this respect, although my research shows that big players are still struggling to glean critical insights from such data resources. Only time will tell, if we are able to match up with the expertise developed in more evolved markets. One advantage for markets like India is that with 'open markets', expert knowledge is creeping into our business ecosystem at a faster rate in recent times.

BROAD CATEGORIES OF ANALYTICAL OUTPUT

Finally, for the sake of completion, I would like to highlight the main areas of analysis required for taking operational decisions for organizations.

Output Consumption Monitoring

The B-school parlance for this activity is 'market research' and 'environment scanning'. Evidently, it is a very important element of monitoring and analysis, to validate current condition of consumption, to ascertain flaws in deployment of current tactics, and to discover new imperatives for the future. Most organizations would have to deploy some system to capture changes in market forces since the essence of business requires calibrating output to ensure compatibility with expected consumption patterns. An important concept in output monitoring to evaluate the organization's performance scorecard is the 'EFFECTIVENESS/EFFICIENCY' measure. Worldwide, firms have struggled to identify inputs that when deployed well can be directly attributable to the output generated by the firm. In this process, the firm is able to identify resources that yield better results compared to others that do not. This way, the firm may be able to achieve better resource mobilization over time and invest in only worthwhile resources (see Box 5.1) that drive business performance (better its efficiency), or be able to identify resources that are able to better business performance significantly (improve effectiveness in deployment).

BOX 5.1 Accounting for Brand Performance Using Prediction Models: A 'Due To' Framework to Measure Effectiveness of Marketing Programmes

Customer Tracking services, such as the ones maintained by large research agencies like ACNielsen and IRI in the United States, provide information not only about consumer attitudes but also their actual behaviour on an ongoing basis. Behavioural data is considered more useful for developing strategy since it directly reflects on business performance rather than conventional slice-in-time customer surveys. This has led to the emergence of marketing research techniques designed for planning future marketing initiatives,

(Box 5.1 continued)

(Box 5.1 continued)

against the more traditional role of merely reporting 'nice-to-know' customer reactions in posterity.

Prediction modelling became a widely used methodology to calibrate marketing mix to positively impact customer response. This trend became popular specifically in the consumer packaged goods (CPG) industry in the United States with large organizations such as Philip Morris, Coke, Pepsi etc., adopting these models for resolving both their strategic and more tactical level decisions.

A very widely used managerial decision support system (DSS) based on prediction modelling of customers' transaction level data is the volume (market share) decomposition analysis. It has evolved over a period into a standard diagnostic tool for marketing managers in developed markets to assess the effectiveness of their marketing programmes. It also helps the manager to evaluate the attractiveness of alternate marketing strategies and therefore is an effective aid in his/her decision-making. The analysis provides a logical basis to the manager to compute the differential impact of firm's advertising strategies and sales strategy vis-à-vis its competitors on the market share of its brands. The total sale of the firm's brand is decomposed into base sales (shown as grey colour area in Figure 5.1) and incremental sales (shown as dotted area in Figure 5.1). The base sale is driven by the long-term equity of the firm and is reflection of its decisions in the past vis-à-vis its competitors. Whereas incremental sales of the firm is influenced by the short-term marketing activity (tactics) of the firm as well as its competitors and helps managers evaluate the effectiveness of various tactics.

The DSS uses the β-coefficients (average impact on sales) of each marketing programme estimated from a sophisticated choice model using statistical techniques such as multinomial logit and regression, to decompose the total brand market

(Box 5.1 continued)

(Box 5.1 continued)

FIGURE 5.1   Decomposition of Volume into Base and Incremental Components

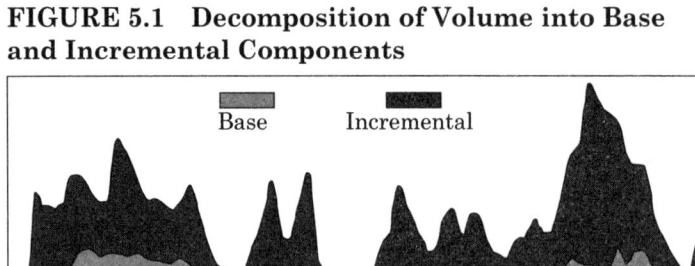

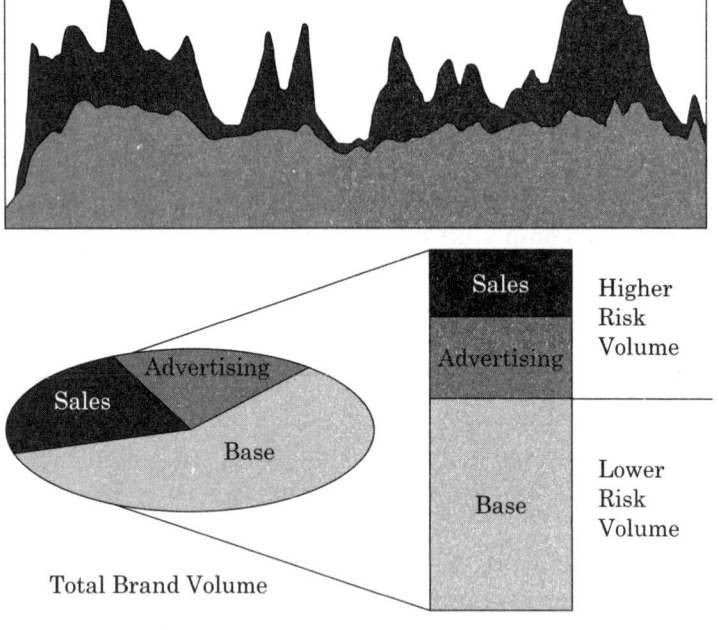

share into individual components that are directly attributable to specific marketing activities (price reductions, promotion packs, freebies, etc.). The consumer choice model is an integral part of developing such DSS and it is extensively used in the marketing research in developed markets to identify real drivers of market performance. Ideally, a choice model requires as an input customer databases covering attributes related to demographic (age, education, etc.), psychometric (attitudes etc.) and marketing mix variables (price, promotion, advertising, display, etc.) of all competing brands in a product category over large number of purchase occasions

(Box 5.1 continued)

(Box 5.1 continued)

from a representative customer sample. Customer Tracking services in the developed markets have developed expertise in collecting and managing these types of data on a continuous basis. Depending on the richness of available data (measured in terms of the number of customer-related and market-related data collected), the incremental sales in Figure 5.1 can further be decomposed to find incremental sales due to price, promotion, trade discounts and short-term advertising or image building effort of the firm (refer Figure 5.2).

FIGURE 5.2   Decomposition of Total Volume to Volume Generated by Each Marketing Mix Element

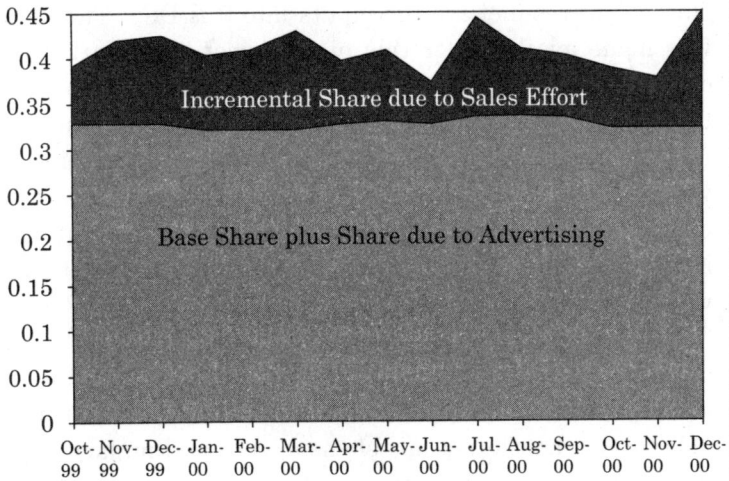

Such decomposition of volume/share into component shares can help manager objectively identify the cause of gain/loss in market share and segregate successful strategies from the rest.

Moreover, it helps in diagnosing the effect of actions taken by competitors in the same period. Development of such

(Box 5.1 continued)

(Box 5.1 continued)

planning tools have had an enormous impact in terms of fine tuning strategic and tactical planning activities in the consumer packaged goods sector in the United States.

A conceptually similar decision support system has been developed recently at the Indian Institute of Management (IIM), Ahmedabad. The system is unique since it is built on consumer panel data available in the Indian market environment. Information from consumer panel maintained by a large research agency which tracks consumer purchases, retail audit information from ORG_MARG which provides pricing and promotional data, and consumers' attitudinal information regarding brands collected from an ongoing survey-based panel are the inputs into this DSS. The data was made available for this pilot project by a marketing organization in FMCG sector. The objective of this pilot was to develop a decision model which would help marketing managers diagnose the impact of brand building initiatives vis-à-vis field level selling initiatives in the overall performance of the brand (market share). It is purported that this is the first step towards building a powerful diagnostic as well as prognostic tool for Indian mangers.

The project replicated the steps described earlier with regards to the estimation of a consumer choice model and subsequent decomposition of the share into parts attributable to each marketing mix element. At a preliminary step, this system can help managers decompose the total market share to base level share and incremental share (refer Figure 5.3).

The incremental share is largely driven by the short-term sales effort of the firm. The ability to decompose total share into components that can be specifically attributed to every marketing tactic used is directly related to the amount of

(Box 5.1 continued)

(Box 5.1 continued)

FIGURE 5.3   Decomposition of Market Share in the Indian Context Based on the Model

Brands	Advertising Spend	Sales Promotion Spend
A	₹10 lakh	₹5 lakh
B	₹2 lakh	₹3 lakh

Market Share

Brand A ████ 40

Brand B ██████ 60

---

details that are captured in the input data regarding the specific marketing activities initiated in the marketplace. Given the limitations in the scope of data collection in the Indian market it is not possible to execute the volume decomposition at the level of granularity obtained with similar types of data collected from the United States. It is anticipated that with improvements in the collection techniques and increase in demand for more detailed record of market level activities, the outputs can be significantly improved.

MANAGERIAL USES OF VOLUME DECOMPOSITION METHODOLOGY

As a diagnostic tool the DSS can help the manager evaluate their periodic investments in various marketing activities vis-à-vis the corresponding performance (volume or market share) attributable to it. Specifically, it helps identify the relative importance of advertising and sales efforts in achieving the ultimate sales. Table 5.1 illustrates an example by which annual expenses incurred in various types of marketing activities are compared with the volume/market share of the brand attributable to the specific activity. This provides

(Box 5.1 continued)

(Box 5.1 continued)

TABLE 5.1   Contribution vs. Efficiency

Marketing Activity	Expenditure (₹ Lacs)	Market Share Impact (%)	Cost Efficiency
TV Advertising	10	30	0.33
Print Advertising	1	2	0.50
Radio Advertising	2	1	2.00
Price Cut	2	1	2.00
Freebee	0.5	2	0.25
Joint Promotion	1	4	0.25

a powerful basis to evaluate marketing activities on an efficiency measure.

It can also foster more efficient resource allocation for future by identifying effective vs. ineffective market development initiatives. As competitive marketing environments become too complex for the manager to evaluate at a holistic level, the model output can provide enough flexibility for the manager to compare alternative strategies after accounting for the complexities in market dynamics. The scenario builder (Figure 5.4) developed on the basis of the model output provides insights about probable outcome due to alternative marketing initiatives for managers to get a 'feel' on what may drive improved performance of their brands. This tool can also evaluate possible competitive reactions to changes in one's own marketing policies. The net result of all changes is portrayed in terms of likely market share of various brands.

Volume (share) decomposition models and their applications have fairly widespread use in the brand and sales management activities of consumer packaged goods companies in the United States. At a generic level, these applications help managers improve the consistency of their

(Box 5.1 continued)

(Box 5.1 continued)

FIGURE 5.4   Scenario Builder

Brands	Advertising Spend	Sales Promotion Spend
A	₹10 lakh	₹5 lakh
B	₹5 lakh ⬆	₹6 lakh ⬆

Market Share

Brand A ▒▒▒▒▒▒▒ 50

Brand B ▒▒▒▒▒▒▒ 50

decisions by acting a 'bouncing board' to validate their own subjective assessments based on their field experience. More specifically, they assist in developing insights about market dynamics in managerial environments where such intuition is lacking. There is, however, the danger of relying too much on the market share forecasts computed by the models on making decisions for the future. Managers must exercise caution while drawing inferences based on the model output since the constraints imposed by the standard techniques of developing mathematical models limit to some extent their 'representativeness' to the real market conditions.

The simplicity of interpretation of volume/share decomposition is the primary reason for its widespread use as a standard tool for making brand and sales management decisions in the United States. Our experience at IIM Ahmedabad in building such models using Indian data has provided some very encouraging results towards developing user-friendly decision support tools.

The relevance of these models in Indian context is beyond doubt. A significant contribution in marketing diagnostics is possible using these models to attribute good (bad) performance to specific functional initiatives such as brand building programmes or ground level sales development activities. While it is easy to point out some negative ramifications

(Box 5.1 continued)

(Box 5.1 continued)

of such management reporting, such as it being used to identify 'scapegoats' in the organization to account for poor performance, it is obvious that the utility of this tool is enormous if used meaningfully to invest in the appropriate market building activities in the long run. Figure 5.3 clearly depicts a real life example of the sales function acting as support to the more significant brand building activities (viewed in terms of proportion of share attributable to each activity group). Our experience shows that this would be true for many product categories in the Indian market where opportunities for market growth and product differentiation are still significant. In the developed markets such as the United States, many product categories exhibit just the opposite characteristic. Market maturity reduces the differentiation across brands and larger proportion of brand market share of leading brands is vulnerable to competitive selling pressures. This fact highlights the predominant role of brand equity building in the Indian context compared to more myopic sales promotional strategies.

Market share decomposition models can be developed for any appropriate geographic market definition—at the country level, a region-specific or city-specific level or even a city-part specific level. The market definition for model development is primarily driven by appropriateness (accounting for the heterogeneity of consumers across various market, and also varied marketing programmes run in various geographic territories) and the availability of adequate consumer data at various defined market levels. If the richness in the data source is adequate, such models can be developed for various customer segment levels (as opposed to geographic markets) to evaluate effectiveness of marketing programmes across various demographic and psychographic segments.

(Box 5.1 continued)

(Box 5.1 continued)

A critical barrier to large-scale usage of these models in India is the non-availability of adequate resource such as a detailed customer database. Managers have expressed interest in such analytical processes and confirm the usefulness of the outputs emanating from such models. However, most organizations lack resources to build large-scale customer databases on their own to initiate such modelling ventures. This is an opportunity for a consortium of like-minded managers across firms to organise and develop a syndicated customer data service for initiating such prognostic marketing research activities.

Note: A version of this article appeared in the *Indian Management*, 42 (1): 86–90.

Input and Process Monitoring

Management students would be familiar with the area of quality management methodologies that essentially ensure compliance of output to the required standards of consumption.

Talent Monitoring

This has to do with the analysis of the skill base of the organization in terms of the valuation of its human resource and the identification of the gaps in the talent base to the requirements of the organization currently and for the future.

It may be prudent to emphasize that 'Analysis' is a good bag of tricks to learn in order to provide support to the fundamental building blocks of managing the organization—*anticipation* and *reaction*. It is used extensively for both prognosis and diagnostic purposes.

But, good analysis is not enough to take sound business decisions.

WHAT IS IMPACTFUL ANALYSIS?

It is fair then to ask the question—what makes a good analysis that supports decision-making well? I can only point as certain elements that I have picked up in my interactions in the classroom, as well as in industry settings. They are very commonplace, yet I suspect are easy to forget in the hurly-burly life of the corporate world.

'Conceptual clarity' is prime most in building good analysis. While all good managers with formal training are adept at the parlance used in formal business education, it is still surprising to many that a simple term such as 'brand equity' may have multiple different interpretations and definitions. Unfortunately, that is the state of the science called 'Management' in today's time. It is therefore pertinent to clarify at the greatest detail what is being defined while making an argument in defence of a proposed business imperative. It is often the cause why many professional conversations have been waylaid by presuppositions that were never specified, and which led to unnecessary roundabout debates in business meetings.

'Familiarity with the context' in which a decision is to be taken is another critical dimension necessary to ensure that the analysis can be honed to suit the circumstances. As stated earlier, very few analyses lead to a perfect solution in a business environment. Hence, it is important to realize the contextual exigencies (if any) to ensure that the conceptual analysis is realistic to the decision-making framework. I remember a case on a Japanese motor car company (Suzuki Samurai[1]) that is taught extensively in some business schools. It is a classic case on segmentation and positioning of a new car for the competitive US market. If the motive of the company is extracting profits from the introduction, the decision on which segment to target would be different than if the company's decision is to first get a foothold in the market through the introduction of this car model. Obviously, then the discussion beyond the concept of segmentation focuses on the real purpose of identifying the 'right' customer for an introductory car model. It is pertinent to look at the time when the introduction was being considered, the nature of competition in the market, the perception of the company in the mind of the customer and more importantly, the cost of a failed introduction (financial loss or more critically, loss of a chance to enter the US market). Conceptualizing the solution therefore requires a heavy dose of contextual constraints and more importantly, the understanding of the decision-maker's 'true' goals and aspirations. Without such grounding, advice on possible solutions becomes somewhat naïve.

---

[1] John A. Quelch and N. Craig Smith, 'Suzuki Samurai: The Rollover Crisis', HBS Case Service: 9-590-127.

DECISION-MAKING AND THE ROLE OF ANALYSIS

> I would not give a fig for the simplicity this side of complexity,
> but I would give my life for the simplicity on the other side
> of complexity.
>
> —Oliver Wendell Holmes

I wish I had a better way of putting it, but I don't. Business schools do not train students to make good decision-makers. No matter how much the employers rue, they just cannot do so. The formal education largely helps in equipping students with decision-making aids—Analysis. Needless to say, the decision-making component of training is a nonstarter since the competence is developed only with *(a)* good familiarity of the background context in which the decision is being taken, and *(b)* consequences to be faced for taking decisions. And that almost never happens in a simulated environment at a training facility. Hence, I would contest the assertion that business schools develop good decision-makers.

'Good apprenticeship' with competent decision-makers is an effective way to build the intuition of decision-making. This is perhaps the reason why many Indian business houses groom their successors internally rather than depend on professional external help. For most of us, having no lineage to such business families, the best bet is to trudge up the decision-making ladder bit-by-bit, judiciously deploying the arsenal of analysis learnt at school and elsewhere. Learning by doing and by making mistakes is the best tutelage for decision-making. Of course, navigational aids learnt at business school make the process somewhat easier.

Six

BRANDING

Is It All About Good Business Acumen?

HOW IS THE 'CURRY' ... GOOD?

A brand is a living entity—and it is enriched or undermined cumulatively over time, the product of a thousand small gestures. We all know that the Disney brand is our most valuable asset. It is the sum total of our seventy-five years in business, of our reputation, of everything that we stand for.

—Michael Eisner, CEO, Disney

Branding has been a raging issue in the realms of management for a long time. It is hotly discussed in business classrooms worldwide and exudes a lot of passion amongst students, especially the ones eyeing a career in marketing and strategy. However, there are many complexities about this concept that are rarely understood with equal clarity as the topic itself. I would like to invest some effort in expressing my opinion about this highly contested domain.

In my parleys with students and practitioners of business principles, I have oftentimes encountered extensive debates regarding the existence of a brand and its importance in building business. In my opinion, and contrary to certain popular notions, a brand is always a consequence of judicious marketing investments that provide a well-rounded and appreciated service to the consumers and markets. I believe that the strength of a brand is only dependent on the organization's push towards positive marketing effort and that there cannot be a separate branding exercise that is unique and different from the design of the marketing offer. In other words, the act of marketing products and services leads to the creation of the brands, strong or weak, depending on how it is finally deciphered by the consumer group.

A brand entity is made up of the following dimensions:

1. An identity or a name that is recalled (identity).
2. A sizable number of consumers know about the existence of the entity (awareness).
3. Its association with unique qualities, both rational and emotional dimensions—where in the strength of the association with the qualities defines the strength of the brand (differentiation).
4. The relevance of the associated quality (benefit) to the consumers' requirements (relevance). See Box 6.1 for an example of irrelevant differentiation.
5. The consistency of the organization in delivering its promise of the associated qualities in its output (fulfilling the promise).

Strong brands are entities whose identity is known to all, their identity is strongly associated with traits (benefits) that are desired by many in the marketplace and these traits are the ones that are difficult to emulate by others. Finally, the entity keeps its promise of delivering the desired benefits without fail on an ongoing basis.

BOX 6.1 Irrelevant Positioning

A tyre manufacturer wanted to differentiate its communication campaign from its competitors. At this time, all major tyre manufacturers focused on product features such as high 'strength', good 'grip', lower 'wear rate', etc., to project their tyres in their advertisements.

This particular tyre company decided to use the emotional plank to advertise its tyres. While consumers are noted to be attached to their vehicles in India, it was assumed that the same emotional connect could be extended to the tyre since it was perceived to be a visible component of the vehicle. Obviously, this ploy was not well researched and the advertising campaign failed to generate the kind of interest that was expected. While the motivation to differentiate from competitor moves was evident, clearly the ploy chosen to do so was inappropriate due to the irrelevance of the association sought.

The final dimension of brand creation is strategically the most critical. While the initial four dimensions are more focused on creating an expectation of a service quality in the mind of the customer, the final one is to do with delivering to the expectation. Strong brands are expected to promise better than average expectations and deliver the same. However, many organizations find it difficult to find a good balance between managing reasonable expectations and delivering against them. Near-term selling pressure in organizations generally motivates managers to hike up promises beyond reasonable level, only to see it come to haunt them later in terms of service failures.

Hence, a strong (weak) brand is consequence of an organization's superior (inferior) performance in delivering its promised service to its markets rather than a separate investment in the creation of an asset. If the marketing initiatives (product features, advertising campaign, service delivery and distribution) are successful, a strong asset (brand) is created. The composition of the brand is largely dependent on the nature of activities initiated in the marketing domain. For instance, a price brand is associated with a bare minimum offer where the price is controlled to be the lowest (or close to it) in the market, whereas a premium brand may have many exotic definitions based on what qualities are being promised.

A potential misconception may arise sometimes when many in practice associate the brand creation with the specific design of the communication campaign that is supposed to create a notion of a brand. Without such association with a strong communication initiative, it is perceived that the brand does not exist. While there is adequate justification in such efforts, it is important to emphasize that mere communication campaign cannot effectively position (or reinforce) the product offered by organizations without a commensurate ratification of the claim by the quality of service meted out by the organization. This is a good reason why McDonald's takes care in ensuring a consistent ambience, product variety and quality, service parameters and outlet design irrespective of where its outlets are located. Off late, it has let go of some consistency to address local environmental sensitivities. A prime example of such relaxation is its entry into India in 1996, when it replaced its traditional burgers (beef patty) with a local substitute (mutton) more conducive and acceptable in the local environment. While such adaptation of global branding strategies for local environments (global strategies) are fairly common, a major concern for marketing strategists is to ensure that adaptations do not stretch beyond acceptable limits so as to inflict permanent damage to the consistency of global associations of the brand.

Historically, the significant role of communication and imagery in enhancing brand perceptions has its moorings in the marketing initiatives of many highly visible consumer products. The role of mass communication initiatives is important in these product categories since the differentiation among alternatives on the core product or service quality is usually marginal (and a hygiene factor) and hence business performance is highly correlated with the ability of firms to differentiate on the perception dimensions based on feelings, emotions and appropriate communication cues.

On the other hand, technologically superior product categories did not require such imagery-based differentiation for long since the basis of customer satisfaction top their delivered services was largely a factor of the product technology and its superiority. Hence, branding (as we have defined it) in such cases was still important, but the mass appeal was caused largely due to the superiority of the core technology and product and not so much by the slickness of the imagery/communication piece. To say that such products were not branded since they were not packaged with an appealing overt communication campaign would be unduly imprudent.

More recently, the importance of communication in brand building has increased in the technology product category, especially with the increased competition in

India and which has diluted the differential product/service advantage that market leaders hitherto had enjoyed. For instance, in the telecom sector, with no major difference in telecommunication capabilities across service providers, imagery-based differentiation has gained heightened attention with the objective to maintain brand salience. But unlike consumer products, telecom managers may have to continue to invest significantly in product/service delivery parameters concurrently to ensure parity in quality of service against competition. Imagery-based differentiation may not be a good substitute for product quality, especially when the quality parameters are highly perceptible and require significant investments to maintain, like in the telecom space.

I am reminded of a seminal work done by Glen Urban[1] and his colleagues at MIT and some others from industry in the eighties, where they compared business performance of the US companies across multiple industries and over decades. They concluded that the dimensions that affected performance positively were: *(a)* How well their services remained differentiated on relevant dimensions over time; *(b)* How intensely they advocated their services in the market; and *(c)* Whether they were the first movers in terms of innovative products and services in the marketplace.

Of the three dimensions, differentiation *(a)* was found to be most effective and intensity of selling *(b)* was second

---

[1]Glen Urban, Theresa Carter, Stephen Gaskin and Zofia Mucha, 'Market Share Rewards to Pioneering Brands: An Empirical Analysis and Strategic Implications', *Management Science*, 32 (1986 June): 645–659.

in effectiveness when compared to the 'first-mover' advantage *(c)* One of the conclusions of this research was that to build good brands (which have profit-bearing capabilities), investment in relevant differentiation provides maximum 'bang for the buck'. This observation has considerable import since it delves into the issue of 'what is a wise investment towards building strong brands'. Obviously, if there are opportunities to create differential positioning for the product/service offer, and if it is relevant to the customer, managers must leverage such opportunities without delay (see Box 6.2). Instead, field-level intense advocacy strategies are mainstay only when effective differentiation is no longer an available option.

In the real world, usually a combination of both selling intensity and differentiation is employed. The resource allocation will obviously depend on the available opportunities to defend a positioning plank vs. the need to enforce visibility of the brand through field-level advocacy programmes.

In conclusion, to reiterate the importance of branding, I would like to describe a typical discussion in a B-school classroom. Usually, when asked to point out reasons for successful performance of an organization, the presence of a strong 'Brand' (product or firm level) is usually offered as an answer by many B-school students. In many ways, that may be the appropriate answer. However, that answer does not provide clues to the route adopted by successful organizations in creating a successful brand. Strong brands are usually synonymous with successful business performance and customer trust, but they need creation through smart marketing management that adheres to the five dimensions of branding stated earlier.

BOX 6.2   Being a Small Manufacturer and a Late Entrant in the Market

In early 2000, I got the opportunity to consult with a medium-sized consumer durable product marketing company. The company had a regional flavour and it had an established presence in its home base. However, like many aspiring and successful companies, it had its focus on becoming a national player.

The national market for the said product was dominated by three major players based in different parts of the county. Obviously, given their scale of operation, their marketing and distribution activity was at a much higher scale than the mid-sized regional player that I consulted with. Clearly, the challenge was how to make a mark in the national market given the size of these competitor companies and the intensity of their marketing activity. The theoretical answer was to look for a specific positioning plank not addressed by the major players, but was, at the same time, perceived to be a relevant benefit by the market segments.

Usually, such opportunities do not exist in highly competitive markets. Even if they do exist, they are not openly visible opportunities. Late comers in the market need to have their 'feet grounded in the market landscape' to be able to perceive such opportunities. Or else, as in the case of my client, focus on the regional base, which was their strength and expand beyond bit by bit over time. There is no antidote for a fast expansion, unless the competitions give way, and they usually do not.

Marketing initiatives are normally a cooperative partnership across different channel partners. Big players normally collude with other big players in the channel. The opportunity to form a respectable partnership for mid-sized companies is to look for neglected members in the channel who would be willing partners in building an alternate product opportunity. In my case, the client had to depend on directly working with Tier 3 and Tier 4 distribution partners, who were usually untouched by the big players.

Hence, brands are a consequence of good marketing ploys, just as business performance, and not an antecedent to profitability.

Finally, like many other investments that take time to fructify and are easy to erode, an effective brand needs nurturing so that the promise of quality service is kept. Any default in the delivery can cause irreparable damage to the value of the brand in the short run (Box 6.3).

BOX 6.3 Building Customer Trust

On his last days in India after a successful corporate stint, an expatriate acquaintance was asked: what would be some of the things he would avoid doing in India, should he have a second stint. To the few obvious ones, he added a striking one: "...I will probably not buy an Annual Service Contract again....can't trust anyone over here to honor a prepaid contract." Somewhat overstated no doubt, but I had to agree that his experience with service standards in India was not an aberration.

Customer service, part of maintaining and enhancing relationship with customers and sustaining a strong Brand, especially after the completion of a sales transaction, is an area with immense opportunities for improvement in many businesses. Not surprisingly, my audiences in the various corporate forums meet this observation with a fair degree of cynicism. While they admit that relationship management is important and has to be ongoing, many retort that organisations lack the stamina to look beyond the immediate horizon when it comes to managing customer satisfaction long term.

The usual suspects for such brittleness range from out-of-sync accountabilities among employees, to the organisation-wide cost efficiency drive that manifests itself in outsourcing

(Box 6.3 continued)

(Box 6.3 continued)

of service functions to low(est) cost "partners". Some even comment that the typical Indian consumer's penchant to extract the most out of a business transaction makes many organisations wary of the extent of relationship they need to maintain. Unfortunately, the last remark is a stark reflection of the low level of trust that customers and organisations have on each other, often referred as an adversarial relationship in traditional marketing literature.

This "mistrust" is best exemplified in the insurance sector where, by the nature of the business dimensions, the "give" and "take" transactions are separated along the temporal dimensions, more in line with the concept of the long term-service contact. Consumer mistrust in the organisation's willingness to honor a commitment (claims processing) is imminent. There is always a doubt whether the sales pitch used to clinch the sale of the insurance cover is in sync with the quality of service delivered when the claims are processed.

This suspicion is heightened because chances are that the customer may have to deal with different entities from the same organisation over different time periods to complete the entire exchange. Such "separated" transactions force many organisations to invest in building and managing trust with customers in the long term, in spite of the several hurdles mentioned earlier. However, trust cannot be built overnight, nor is it advisable to take giant strides all at once. Instead, it is best to crawl bit by bit towards a higher order relationship with the customer. This relationship thrives on reciprocity, something best managed if both parties show willingness to build it incrementally.

The difficult part in this process is the initiation of these confidence-building measures. A good way to start will be by recalibrating the selling function. Traditionally, selling

(Box 6.3 continued)

(Box 6.3 continued)

has been synonymous to building customer expectations, unrealistic at times, just to ensure that the initial exchange process takes place. When the back-end service does not match the exaggerated claims made in the selling process, long term damage to brand equity is inevitable.

Harmonisation of the selling and service processes to ensure that customer expectations are "managed within reasonable bounds and satisfied comprehensively" is the key to maintaining viable long term business relationships. In a nutshell, can we effectively engineer a "human face" to our selling process and back it up with a "machine-like" efficiency in our service infrastructure? Maybe competitive forces over time will enforce such stricter regimen.

Source: This initially appeared in *Hindustan Times.*[2]

In a nutshell, the brand(s) of a firm encapsulate all the good (bad) management practices employed by the firm over time. It is therefore a very good reflection of the strength of the business enterprise. Here, I would just like to refer to the research project that resulted in the book *Built to Last* by Jim Collins and co-author Jerry I. Porras,[3] where they traced the growth trajectory of some companies, formerly startups and then to becoming titans over time.

Marriott hotels started out with a single A&W root beer stand. George Merck had a family apothecary before Merck & Co. became a pharmaceutical giant. Starbucks had five stores for

---

[2]Arindam Banerjee, 'Building Customer Trust', *Hindustan Times*, 14 February 2008.

[3]Jim Collins and Jerry I. Porras, *Built to Last: Successful Habits of Visionary Companies* (USA: Harper Business, 2004).

13 years, and Nike took years before it broke $1 million in revenue. The only thing overnight about Walmart's success was the public's awareness. For the first seven years, Sam Walton had two stores.

Hence, there is overwhelming evidence that great brands are not made overnight but actually are the result of good business acumen over a long, rather a long, long time.

Seven

SOME STRAY THOUGHTS ON EFFECTIVE MANAGEMENT PRACTICE

THE GARNISH

I realize that I have almost come to the end of my 'curry making' guide for business management. While I have taken care, to the best of my ability, to make my arguments complete and to the point, I cannot ignore some important dimensions of management practices that do not necessarily fit into the overall flow of my exposition. They are nevertheless important to be included in the manuscript. Consider them to be garnish that you would add on your curry to improve the flavour and taste—a dash of herbs or bit pieces of nuts, just to provide that extra zing to the taste buds. Without their judicious application, the organizations may be managed well, but they are still worth a consideration.

I present them to you in no particular order of importance, nor do I suggest that the reader subscribe to them. These are views based on my personal experience and have served me well over the years.

HIRING A CONSULTANT FOR DECISION-MAKING

Never trust anyone you don't understand.

—Jack Trout

I have a strong view on this one, having been a consultant myself to many organizations in the past decade and a half. Don't hire one, if possible and if you do have to, don't get into the habit of depending on them for too long.

Consultants are hired for various reasons—cost arbitrage, expertise not worth investing internally, outsider's perspective, solving an internal political battle and the sheer comfort of delegating the responsibility of decision-making to someone else. It is the last one that is a dangerous habit. Like a shrink, a consultant can many times become an easy route for internal competency and acumen to erode away, to the sheer delight of many consultants, since it increases the prospect of future business.

Prudence would suggest that consultants be used to provide knowledge and competence in the short run (unless they are consciously hired as an economically viable substitute for internal resources) to equip decision-makers with the expertise they require. However, continued dependence on the external expert for assistance is something that requires review to ensure that the management competency within does not go into a paralysis mode.

INVEST IN GOOD AND STABLE WORKFORCE

Companies ... have a hard time distinguishing between the cost of paying people and the value of investing in them.

—Thomas A. Stewart (1948–)
US journalist and author in *Intellectual Capital* (1997)

Practically nothing can substitute for good quality work force in organizations—critical people (who really run the organization) cannot be substitutable. The other way to state is that the human brain behind successful organizations is not dispensable and no process, technology or otherwise can really work as well. Investment in good people takes time and requires endurance since 'it ain't going to happen overnight'. But, at the risk of repeating, I must emphasize that eroding good workforce does not take too long. It is therefore very necessary to ensure proper investment in talent and capability and to maintain the same over an extended period of time. Good leadership in organizations requires not only to develop adequate capabilities, but also to ensure that the same are handed over generations of managerial talent that will follow in the future.

RISING UP OVER FUNCTIONAL PRIDE TO FOCUS ON ORGANIZATIONAL GOALS

The business organization is one integrated entity and there is a common objective to excel on prescribed performance metric. Functional objectives (sales targets, recruitment targets, etc.) are necessarily derivatives of the overall organizational goals and hence by themselves do not directly serve to achieve overall goals. Large organizations are faced with additional challenges of motivating employees to focus on the global objectives of the organization, rather than merely their functional ones. This is not to belittle the necessity of managing functional goals, but to emphasize that it is only part of the responsibilities that organizational managers need to assume.

A good operations manager must, some day, look beyond the immediate responsibility of delivering output at the lowest cost and permissible quality. Organizations over time would demand that they also adapt processes to innovate and create output that is compatible with evolving times. This may require a deeper understanding of customer and market data, which may reveal the opportunities to improve service delivery over time. Similarly selling as a function has evolved over the years from a pure target-driven transactional interaction with customers wherein raising expectations was considered the route to clinch the deal, to a more mature long-term investment in human relationships based on mutual trust and respect. It is no longer proper to meet sales targets by being aggressive on setting expectations of prospective customers, only to 'let them down' when delivering the promise. In today's competitive times, such pathetic conduct can only result in bad 'word of mouth' in no time.

MANAGING DEMAND IS DIFFICULT, BUT IMPORTANT

Among the various dimensions that affect the company's fortunes, this one has the most uncontrollable dimensions. The reason is quite obvious. Many elements of demand creation are affected by exogenous forces such as environment, consumer and competition, things that are not as much under the control of the organization, whereas controlling internal costs to affect short-term profitability is relatively simpler.

This is perhaps the reason why both management consultants and internal leadership tend to focus more on cost control to show near-term direct impact of their efforts on profitability. Investments on demand creation, while critical for long-term survival, may not prove to be a very reliable and 'worthy' investment in the short run, for reasons cited earlier. My suspicion is that typically organizations spend far more time trying to 'fix' profitability and related performance measures by managing cost control (Box 7.1). I vividly remember a problem-solving engagement where we were faced with the adverse impact of cost rationalization done by the organization, in this instance a steel rolling mill. Standardizing sizing of output can reduce setting time in a steel rolling mill, which has direct impact on production cost reduction. Unfortunately, standardization in output standards can also negatively impact demand especially when the customer requirements are heterogeneous and somewhat inflexible to such reduction in available product variety from the supplier. In this particular instance, although the product items were 'weeded out' based on demand considerations (low requirement), what was ignored was that there were critical requirements from preferred customers and their non-availability created considerable ill will in the market over time.

Foresighted organizations and their leadership spend more time in long-term investments in market development as well. As stated in an earlier chapter, investments that require longer lead time to fructify are best initiated when organizations are flushed with funds and need not worry about immediate returns on their new investments. Complacency has no place even in prosperous times in such organizations.

BOX 7.1 Customer Focus—Is This Rocket Science? Views from a Harassed Customer*

Try walking into an office of any small time entrepreneur, businessman or trader. Chances are that you may find a slogan adorning the reception area – "Customer satisfaction is our motto". Nothing profound in that, many of us have sometimes seen such slogans prominently on advertisements and billboards for decades. The more business- savvy types have dispensed with it long ago, categorizing it as cliché and not in tune with times.

What is not so clichéd and ordinary is the fact that very few of our business practitioners have actually molded their profession around this philosophy – knowingly or unknowingly. Let me explain – have you as a customer been subjected to sales calls by DSAs (Direct Sales Agents) of reputed banks proclaiming that you are the lucky one who has been cleared for a loan of some preposterous amount. Yes indeed, most of us have at some point or the other. You decide to be polite and decline the offer in the most affable manner and hope that it is the end of your transactions with the bank's sales agent. Think again – high probability that for the next several days you shall get multiple calls from similar direct sale personnel of the so-called reputable bank, all offering the same product that you had declined just the other day. You may be lucky not to have them visit your home or office, again offering the same product. When you confront them with the fact that someone had already approached you from their office earlier with a similar offering and that you have declined it for the umpteenth time, they feign ignorance and unashamedly blame it on some internal operational gaffe which they are not responsible for.

Ultimately, your patience runs out and you threaten to complain about them, terminate your existing business transactions with the bank, and then they may let you go. Only for a brief period, and then the calls start all over again.

(Box 7.1 continued)

(Box 7.1 continued)

As the quintessential customer, I reflect with much worry on these countless experiences with direct selling campaigns where my ego is supposedly being pampered by offering to me products and services meant for the "select few", I wonder whether it is worth being the prime customer to these reputable companies – am I really so important for them to make me feel "happy" or, are they just hounding me for being a representative of the "good" (read: profitable) customer segment.

As a management academic, it appears to me to be too gross to be called anything that implies "Customer Focus". Are we building brands by being in "hot pursuit" of our so called customers, by employing under trained, and unsensitized front office personnel (DSAs), or simply destroying the goodwill that our reputable organizations have in the minds of the ordinary consumers? One really can't tell the real reasons are for such sloppy implementation of marketing theory.

Across markets, customer-centrism is mostly driven by the motivation to fight intense competitive pressures. Sustainable differentiation, also packaged as "Unique Selling Proposition", is the mantra of successful marketing firms who have managed to tide over competitive onslaughts to preserve their market share and dominance. In fact for many years, one of the only few service industries in the United States that got away with sloppy service was the cable TV service providers, primarily because they were the few who enjoyed territorial monopoly.

In India, we have moved quite far away from the controlled economy of the decades prior to the nineties. Market reforms over the past fifteen years, has injected a high dose of competitive pressures in many industry sectors. Be it telecom, retail financial services, organized retailing or airline, competitive pressures have crept in at rapid pace and sources of inherited product differentiation are rare and hard to find.

(Box 7.1 continued)

(Box 7.1 continued)

In spite of these difficult times for suppliers of goods and services, it is rare that one finds cases of near perfect execution of customer service principles, to the point where the predominant perception among customers is one of satisfaction rather than harassment.

The impact is rather disappointing to society at large. Customers like, myself, come away fretting and fuming about the lack of decent business interactions in the form of efficient service. Some other customers (and I suspect a significant lot) resign themselves to this sub standard fare expecting no redemption from it. Suppliers are in no better shape since their "not-so-hot" service offerings forces them to lower prices in order to keep attracting customers.

For example, think telecom and one cannot avoid perceiving the fairly high occurrence of poor quality phone connections compounded with jammed circuits, interference and static. At the same time, mobile phone charges have steadily reduced because of the competitive onslaught which has severely affected the financial performance of all service providers. Some industry experts will contend that the phenomenon was initiated with sudden rise in competition which led to a spate of customer acquisition by most service providers in order to reduce service costs. What followed as a consequence of this volumes game was the adoption of sub-standard service-quality norms and a market splurged with price promotions from suppliers. One wonders whether the Indian market is really nothing but acutely price sensitive as many management practitioners make it out to be—aren't there enough consumers willing to pay a little bit more, if only the customer service was more timely, reliable and cordial.

While I have no accurate reaction to my seemingly rhetorical question, I am quite sure about the fact that customers are simply unwilling to pay more for what is dish out

(Box 7.1 continued)

(Box 7.1 continued)

in today's world in the name of customer service. What is uncertain is that whether they would willingly pay more for better service, the latter unfortunately is not easily available in today's world.

The point that I am driving at is simply the following— What will it take for our organizations to be effectively focused on the real customer needs as required by her? I can propose the following as opportunity areas to reflect on:

1. **Are we doing enough consumer research?**
   This does not just imply using the scientific market research tools taught at B-schools. What I mean is whether the corporate sector is investing enough time on the field to decipher the real lacuna in the consumer needs. I have grave doubts about their involvement with actual consumer research. In my opinion, simply relying on third-party reports such as the ones supplied by market research agencies is not enough. Managers ought to get out of their offices and must "walk the markets" on a regular basis, just to feel and get sensitized. I do not think enough "walking" is done yet. Instead it is substituted by a mish-mash of internal research, learnings from the occident (read: America/Europe) and pure gut-feel. According to me, among the three, the latter is the most beneficial so long as it is based on relevant past experience.

2. **Are we paying enough attention to the details?**
   Here's a place where we have traditionally faltered. Many people have stated that we are a nation of great planners, but not great implementers. Many examples from recent corporate ventures will validate this fact. I remember having visited a new book store (part of nationwide retail chain) in the city of Ahmedabad some

(Box 7.1 continued)

(Box 7.1 continued)

years ago. The store had been recently opened and had all the ingredients of a new-age bookstore – attractive frontage, a great selection, a coffee counter, ample reading area, bright interior lighting, a children's area – in all a great place to spend a day during the weekend browsing through books with the family. Except for one small irritant – the check out attendant's demeanor did not synergize with the new-age ambience. Obviously, the management did not feel it necessary to invest in the software (attendant's professional behaviour) as it did in the hardware (store infrastructure). The staffer's acerbic behaviour, perhaps a legacy from his past work life, was completely out of synchronization with the plush décor of the store interior. He was completely incompetent to handle the various sensitive inter personnel complications that someone in his position could face. It was clear to me that the store management had decided to skimp on what, from the point of the customer, should have been one of the most critical elements of service – professional attitude of the store attendants. How many of us would tolerate rude behaviour from suppliers unless we have no choice? Needless to say, I beat a hasty retreat from this snazzy bookstore, never to return.

In our hurry to implement new projects, perhaps we need to remember to induct in our project teams members who at least have the luxury to revisit operational details just to make sure things are "right" – someone who acts as an auditor, certifier and at times a whistle-blower. Believe me, it helps having a party pooper on board, while the rest of us perfect that art of "shooting from the hip", especially if the consequence of a party going horribly bad is pretty enormous.

(Box 7.1 continued)

(Box 7.1 continued)

3. **Are we still looking only at efficiency parameters when we manage our customer relationships?**
   Unfortunately, that appears to be very true. Old habits die hard. It appears that our decades old supplier-side orientation still creeps into our decision making. A few years ago, a business manager of a credit card company was discussing the ways and means of improving his customer complaint management initiatives. This was the era just before the advent of the toll free customer care numbers. An innocuous advice to him to be the pioneer in India by establishing an all-India toll free customer care number was received with heightened skepticism. The problem was then and still is the same – any customer-focused initiative attracts a significant dent in the corporate coffers. Sure it is costly to install a toll free number, but what is difficult to measure is the effectiveness of such measure. No one is sure what will be the impact on the demand side. Hence, the tendency to look at controlling costs which obviously has a direct impact on the bottom line.

   What may confound the purpose of this efficiency driven profit model are, *(a)* the fact that cost reductions generally have a limit (even if you find creative ways to reduce them) and, *(b)* incessant cost reduction measures can many times have negative impact on the market demand and may pull down the results of the profitability model. The latter point needs a little more explanation.

   In recent times, I have been assisting the management of a large process-driven plant in developing their near term marketing activities. The plant has recently undergone significant cost rationalization through control measures which has also led to a rationalization

(Box 7.1 continued)

(Box 7.1 continued)

of the output product portfolio. The management was obviously quite pleased with the results of the cost cutting measures. However, the repercussion of a smaller product portfolio was apparent from the fairly widespread negative market reaction. Qualitative analysis of the markets revealed that there was evidence of significant inroads being made by competitors with the specific organization having exited some fairly big customer segments. The product rationalization exercise solely driven by operating cost control measures had not really analyzed the implication of the same on demand dynamics, resulting in possible negative impact on performance in the long term. Demand analysis is perceived by many to be more difficult to conduct prior to implementation of a new initiative and hence by-passed many times at high costs.

In a nutshell, I think there is a need to develop the discipline of studying markets and customers diligently. The discipline and thoroughness of the exercise is more important than the mere act of going through the motions. Local market immersion exercises for managers are oftentimes discussed, but rarely implemented studiously in most organizations.

Ideas and notions from the occident are good starting points many times to evolve smashing indigenous products and services, but they can never fully substitute for local market immersion exercises and consequent indigenous strategy development. Unfortunately, here's one area we definite lack competency. The focus appears to be more towards quick adaptation of ideas already operational in more evolved markets – hence, the plethora of cross-selling initiatives, promo-wars and glitzy infrastructure in terms of

(Box 7.1 continued)

(Box 7.1 continued)

malls and new-age retail outlets with scant regard for the expectations of the poor Indian customers. As customers of the new millennium, surely we deserve better treatment.

*A version of this article appeared in the *Indian Management*, August 2005.

BOX 7.2 Data Acquisition Plan: The Road Map to Successful CRM Type Strategy*

About a decade ago, marketing research industry in the United States seemed poised to take off on an altogether new technological flight. Research clients in manufacturing and marketing organisations of customer goods and services seemed to readily accept the notion that strategy building needed some significant inputs from customer data collected from tracking services. These data were different from the ones supplied until then by research suppliers through one off survey analysis.

Tracking services supplied information not only about consumer attitudes but also their actual behaviour, that too on an ongoing basis. Behavioural data was considered more useful for developing strategy since it provided true insights about customer's likes and dislikes rather than slice-in-time customer surveys which provided stated preferences. This led to the genesis of using marketing research techniques as a planning tool for the future rather than using it to merely report "nice-to-know" customer reactions in posterior. Strategy development exercises turned more data savvy and scientifically tuned and corporate America was talking precision in estimated earnings rather than simply directions. Prediction modelling was in vogue and calibration of marketing mix to affect appropriate customer response was necessary, mere directional insights

(Box 7.2 continued)

(Box 7.2 continued)

were not enough. Large marketing organisations such as Kraft, Pepsi, Coke, General Mills and the like invested in customer data management initiatives, recruited and trained technicians to mine the databases and focussed on interpreting past customer behaviour along with individual characteristics to fine tune marketing strategies directed at specific customer groups. This technique became popularly known as micro marketing based on data analysis.

The emphasis on customer data analysis and the subsequent use of the analytical output for strategy building evolved more dramatically in the banking services sector where the preponderance of customer transaction data is overwhelming. The entire business of banking services is about building and maintaining individual customer relationship through value-added customer service. This spurred the need for developing individualised customer care strategies to ensure that each customer (at least the high value ones) was kept satisfied perpetually. Customer retention was important especially in the context of high competition, which was prevalent in the western markets. The route to ensure high degree of satisfaction was to devise individualised strategies for every important customer. Thus evolved the concept of customer relationship management (CRM) which not only incorporated the micro-marketing strategies based on data analysis but advanced further to customise marketing efforts to individual customers based on past behaviour.

Similar CRM strategies evolved in several service-based industries, which have the access to large-scale transaction data of individual customers. Goods and services that lend themselves to repeated usage and require the customer to directly access the provider to make a purchase are amenable

(Box 7.2 continued)

(Box 7.2 continued)

to CRM type strategies. In order to build a database of information of customer transaction, adequate computing infrastructure is required to identify and store individual transactions.

DEVELOPING EFFECTIVE CRM-TYPE STRATEGIES

In order to devise effective strategies based on past customer behaviour, a thorough understanding of each customer with respect to his/her profile, and past consumption pattern is required. While this may sound fairly prosaic, there are some significant operational issues to plan for organisations resorting to CRM initiatives. These can be categorised as:

1. Customer data acquisition from all customer contact points,
2. Data mining for building customer insights and prediction modelling,
3. Developing appropriate initiatives on a proactive basis to improve customer satisfaction.

Perhaps the core of this process is the development of a data acquisition plan and its implementation. The quality of the raw material used to develop customer insight determines the ultimate effectiveness of any strategy. The subsequent stages in the CRM process development are of secondary importance. Yet, there are many instances of organisations investing less in the planning of data acquisition rather they bank on efficient data mining initiatives to drive their CRM initiatives. Unfortunately, this has resulted in less than marginal success of many such initiatives.

(Box 7.2 continued)

(Box 7.2 continued)

THE CASE OF DEBT COLLECTION FROM THE RETAIL BANKING SECTOR

To substantiate this point, a case of an implementation of a customised debt collection initiative at a credit card company (bank) in the United States is presented here. The objective of this CRM initiative was to identify and assign appropriate delinquent customers to a litigation process to accelerate collection of pending dues from them. It was estimated that this method would significantly improve the debt collection amount of the bank since it had over $5–6 billion of delinquent balance. According to the bank, all delinquent customers were not suitable to be coerced into paying their dues. Delinquent customers, who had pending disputes with the bank or had a genuine grievance, were definitely not candidates for litigation. Hence, there was a need to search the history of past interactions of customers with the bank and deselect customers with such records.

After deselecting the cases with dispute or grievance, a second stage classification was attempted to segregate appropriate customers for litigation. The logic used was that it would be viable to send only those delinquent customers who would pay up only when litigation proceedings were initiated against them. Past behaviour and profiling information was required to identify this segment. It was presumed that customers who were unwilling to pay up their dues, but had the ability to pay would generally satisfy the criteria for selection for litigation. Hence, it was necessary to determine the financial solvency of the delinquent customers in order to identify the appropriate cases for litigation. Available customer information regarding possession of assets or a job that fetches a steady income is suitable to make this assessment.

(Box 7.2 continued)

(Box 7.2 continued)

Unfortunately, this type of information is not readily available with most banks for a variety of reasons. First, they may not have instituted a procedure to collect this information at the time when customers apply for credit cards. Some banks do have procedures to collect information about customer's income. However, this information is not updated on a periodic basis since there are no instituted procedures to monitor changes in financial status of customers over time. Also, there are instances of data corruption causing a high level of missing information in the databases. As a result of the non-availability of appropriate information, identification of customers to be sent to litigation becomes non-trivial. Less than perfect information about customers imposes constraints on the identification of the right candidates for litigation.

Similar problem was encountered at the bank while attempting to reengineer the debt collection practices. Decision tree analysis was employed based on available surrogate information such as past behavioural data of customers, in lieu of information on the customer's financial status, which predicted who would be a likely candidate to be sent to arbitration. Instead of definitively identifying financially solvent cases, statistical modelling was used to predict true financial solvency of delinquent customers with the help of the information of their past behaviour. Cases with high probability of being sound financially were assigned to the litigation process.

It was not viable to assign all delinquent cases to litigation because of the significantly high cost associated with the litigation proceedings. There is a $100 court fee for filing every case for litigation. The result of developing sophisticated prediction models was just about average. The bank was able to identify about 40% of the true cases that were appropriate for litigation. Even with a very comprehensive search across

(Box 7.2 continued)

(Box 7.2 continued)

multiple databases in the organisation, the bank was unable to improve the identification process using the sophisticated prediction-modelling tool. The silver lining was that given the scale of operation at the bank, even with this moderate success in customer identification process it was able to save over $40 million annually.

This illustration is not an isolated case of low to moderate success in developing successful business strategies based on customer information. Based on the author's experience from the banking sector in the United States, no major bank in the past five years has recorded high degree of successes in formulating customer transaction data driven business strategy (with the possible exception of Capital One).

While it is conceptually very appealing to devise track consumers and fine tune future strategies based on an understanding of their past behaviour, many organisations have yet to evolve internal processes that can capture and bank appropriate customer information for future use. Unfortunately this remains the major roadblock in the effective implementation of CRM or database driven strategy initiatives. The stress is on the appropriateness of the data captured and not on the scale. The experience of the banking industry in the United States has exhibited the importance of strategic planning of data acquisition for its effective use in the future. Without such proactive steps, managers will have to reconcile themselves to moderate successes in database led strategy development initiatives.

KEY ISSUES IN SUCCESSFUL IMPLEMENTATION OF CRM INITIATIVES

Traditionally, the technology and systems group in the organisation has spearheaded information acquisition and

(Box 7.2 continued)

(Box 7.2 continued)

management. In reality, this tends to be a hurdle since there is a significant disconnect between the tasks of data management and, data use for strategic purpose. The former is handled by the more technology savvy IT and systems personnel in organisations who may not be looped in with the mainstream business functions of the organisation. While management and development of databases and information flow grid is strategically important, the responsibility of ensuring the acquisition of good quality of information based on their potential applicability to strategy development activities has to be assumed by the user groups. Ideally, this would mean that the prime movers of a CRM strategy in an organisation should be the line functionaries, such as, marketing, finance or operations, who would benefit most from an effective database driven business initiative.

Hence it is important that firms initiate a planning process for acquiring appropriate information resources prior to investing enormous amounts of funds on development of database management systems. Proactive planning by line managers regarding their future information needs should ensure tracking of the required information resources that will drive effective business strategy.

Strategic CRM initiatives will require the following:

1. User groups in organisations must develop a proactive plan to capture appropriate customer information.
2. This plan must be implemented by the systems and technology group, which includes customer tracking and data management issues.
3. Appropriate data mining activities need to be planned by the user group to support various customer management strategies as required in a timely manner. This activity will be supported by the systems group.

(Box 7.2 continued)

(Box 7.2 continued)

> 4. User groups need to develop appropriate customer development strategies based on the insights available from the data mining exercise.
>
> The general conclusion reached is that effective usage of customer data for developing business strategies will require more active participation by the line managers in the entire CRM development process. In reality, this remains an illusionary goal. In the banking sector in the United States, most CRM based strategies are still driven by systems and IT functions with low involvement of the actual user groups. One would suspect that the scenario is not very different in other industries.
>
> ## RETAIL BANKING SECTOR IN INDIA: DEVELOPMENT OF CRM INITIATIVES
>
> Not surprisingly, India is still at a preliminary stage in the systems development cycle with respect to CRM strategies, compared to other developed markets. This is a boon in more than one way since it provides Indian managers an opportunity to learn and avoid the loopholes identified in more developed markets.
>
> Based on a limited survey of the Indian retail-banking sector, we are able to classify organisations based on their CRM initiatives into three categories:
>
> 1. *The "transplants":* Many foreign banks operating in the Indian market have adopted syndicated CRM processes that have been developed by their principals in more developed western economies. Most bank

(Box 7.2 continued)

(Box 7.2 continued)

managers in this group admit that the success rate of their CRM strategies is at best moderate. They also have no significant plans to customise such processes for the Indian market primarily because of perceived low marginal benefit. This is mainly because of the low degree of competition in the Indian market that does not make it viable for foreign banks to invest in customising their CRM processes for India.

2. *The "performers":* Among the "Indian managed" banks, this group has acquired the so-called first mover advantage of cornering the profitable premium segment of the customers. Several large privately held and quasi-nationalised banks fall in this group. High performance has generated large fund surplus, which bestows a high degree of confidence among the managers of these banks. Early initiatives at targeting premium customers along with low levels of competition from other banks are the prime reasons for their good performance. However, managers of these banks have no reason to be complacent. With growing levels of competition, single segment focus may not remain an effective strategic option in the medium term. Micro-marketing strategies driven by consumer insights will determine successful businesses of the future. Therefore, in order to remain market leaders, these banks have to equip themselves with appropriate technology to track and analyse customer behaviour. A more challenging task will be to reorient managers to think of customers at the micro-segment level or even at the individual level rather than as a single large entity.

3. *The "followers":* Many domestic banks, both private and state-run, fall in this category. Not having had

(Box 7.2 continued)

(Box 7.2 continued)

the benefit of the first mover advantage that the "performers" have, they are reconciled to build competitive advantage by developing CRM-type infrastructure in their organisations to target micro segments and provide customised value proposition, which the "performers" have not yet initiated. From a systems life cycle perspective, they are ahead of the "performers" on two major dimensions. First, they have realised the need to fine-tune the marketing strategy towards micro segments or even to the extent of looking at individual customers. Second, most of these banks have started collating the transaction data from all customer "touch points". As pointed out earlier, this exercise in data management is fallacious since it is driven primarily by the systems group in many banks without significant involvement of the line functionaries.

Managers at one such "follower" organisation, a large quasi-nationalised bank, pointed out that the primary responsibility of CRM activities was wrested with the technology group of the bank. Data collation from various customer service points was the most significant task that the technology group was currently engaged in. The general perception was that issues related to possible strategic use of data and information use were of secondary nature, since the primary activity was to get the data organised. It was clear that the management had adopted a sequential approach to CRM development. Significant investments had been made in developing data "conduits" for transfer and storage of data without much attention given to the quality and nature of data being organised. The team leader of the technology group recognised this as a drawback, but he expressed his

(Box 7.2 continued)

(Box 7.2 continued)

---

inability to develop a more collusive CRM initiative with the involvement of the line functionaries.

According to him, some organisational hurdles impeded the formation of a constructive collusion among the various functional managers of the bank. First, there was a general lack of awareness regarding the mechanics of executing CRM based strategies in the organisation, especially among the managers who are responsible for customer interface. While most recognised the need to customise product offerings to retain customers, the process of gathering and analysing customer data to develop insights for building strategy was perceived to be too technical and beyond their purview.

There was also a political dimension that seemed to have caused obstacles in healthy CRM implementation. Given the heavy reliance on technology for building CRM capabilities, the systems group was the natural choice for championing such initiatives. This may have been perceived by other managers in organisations, albeit erroneously, as a personal turf of a functional group and hence may not have spurred active participation by them. Till date, the impact of the CRM related activities on the bank's performance remains unclear since the development of the various processes is still on. However, the top management has definitely concluded that any potential gains would be limited for the reasons cited above.

I suspect that the above reasons could be attributed to the lack of unison in planning CRM initiatives in many other organisations. This has serious implications since the banking sector in India can ill-afford to spearhead a costly data management initiative for CRM related activities without proper planning of potential use of the information resources.

(Box 7.2 continued)

(Box 7.2 continued)

FROM TECHNOLOGY TO CUSTOMER: A SHIFT IN PERSPECTIVE

It is quite evident that technology is not the focus of a CRM initiative in an organization. It is also amply clear that technology has a significant role to play in ensuring smooth implementation, but effective strategy development requires a thorough understanding of customer behaviour. This is possible by tracking customer responses to past and current marketing initiatives, developing insights about key customer groups, be wary of changing trends in customer preferences observed from their past behaviour and finally to use this knowledge base to judiciously to develop segment-level strategies to enhance business performance.

This requires a more broad-based employment of organisational resources compared to what is presently being deployed. Effective CRM type initiatives will have to be led by functional areas which have the most interaction with the customer, i.e., the marketing function. Marketing managers therefore need to be more technology savvy to employ the current tools for data management and tracking, integrate their knowledge about customers with careful collection and analysis of appropriate historical transaction data to evolve better customer specific product offerings.

The mantra for long term viability of CRM led initiatives in organisations is obvious:

1. Involve the line managers in the data collection and management initiatives.
2. Think of customer data as an investment in the future. Evolve a dynamic plan to capture the "right" data over time.

(Box 7.2 continued)

(Box 7.2 continued)

> 3. Be customer focussed. The CRM software is often one of the many dimensions to achieve customer focus.
>
> Fortunately, commitment to CRM initiatives in India is still fairly insignificant. It is therefore important for Indian business organisations to avoid pitfalls as uncovered by the experiences in more developed economies. This would significantly improve returns on investments made in this area.
>
> *A version of this article appeared in the *Indian Management* in July 2002.

THE WIRED WORLD OUTSIDE AND INSIDE

I learnt this bit the hard way. In spite of the scientific and professional veneer, business dealings across the world are still closely controlled through networks, especially in the critical and high value turfs. Competency, rationality and scientific acumen matter, but are not enough to clinch the best deals. Somewhere in this global economic quagmire, there exists an informal nexus of power that controls all important dealings. This is ever so true internally within large organizations. In many instances, the informal power nexus transcends beyond the formal organizational hierarchy. While such happenings are not uncommon and in many ways are manipulated for individual gains, it is fair to comment that informal power nexus are also worthwhile to tap to drive progressive initiatives within large organizations. I would coin this phenomenon—'good political manoeuvring' in organizations, especially large organizations with necessarily elaborate procedures which do not allow radical ideas to fructify so easily. The important thing for business executives who want to make a mark is to identify appropriately the informal power nexus, align themselves with it and affect good organizational change by ethical means. I want to make sure that the reader does not misconstrue my views over here. What has been described over here is oftentimes associated with political wheeling—dealing with negative connotations. For a fact, that is true in many large enterprises across the world. Politicking is generally associated with negative emotions; however, it is my firm belief that when the objectives are noble, some amount of political manoeuvring to cut corners in order to achieve objectives through the informal route may be advisable so long as it is for the long-term good of the enterprise. As a practice it has recorded good results, except given its controversial trappings such methods have never been formally documented. My recommendations may certainly open the debate on whether noble objectives justify any means to achieve them. I shall table that debate for another day.

There could also be a counterargument to the above assertions. The assumption that large organizations are necessarily lethargic due to their cumbersome procedures could be questioned and one can necessarily seek avenues to create better effectiveness in decision-making. Unfortunately, the reality is that scale and effectiveness are counter-correlated. With large scale, organizational leash is required to ensure coordinated action among all constituents. This is the genesis of lethargy or sluggishness/weariness that can set the precedence of demotivation among individual employees. For this particular reason, applying the concept of 'good politicking' may be appropriate to get the top management galvanized to take effective action recommended by smart rankers within the organization. With globalization, the network intensity will increase. In my opinion, understanding and leveraging this networked economy and avoiding its pitfalls will be a critical skill that business managers and entrepreneurs of the future will have to assimilate for successful business performance.

EFFECTIVE BUSINESS COMMUNICATION MATTERS

If your words or images are not on point, making them dance in color won't make them relevant.
—Edward Tufte, Professor Emeritus, Yale University

This may sound corny, but it is still worth repeating a million times over. More so in the context of our Indian schooling system that emphasizes the virtues of analysis, but does significantly less when it comes to training their pupils on communicating with logical reasoning. Making cogent arguments to support a business alternative can go a long way in establishing credibility of the employee early in the professional curve. It is therefore important not only to have sufficient fluency in the language of business communication (English is widely used in corporate India), but also to have expertise in structuring the communication in a way that sounds logically convincing. This is worth delving into a bit and consequently the section is going to be comparatively long and seemingly 'tedious'. But, given the relative scarcity of this competency in India, it is worth the trouble of describing it in some detail.

Many business communication documents appear to have: *(a)* too much process, *(b)* no business context, *(c)* too much analysis but little or no answers to business questions and *(d)* no main message or purpose of the communication. Hence, under these circumstances, communication tends to be 'purposeless', excruciatingly boring and hard to decipher. Having spent many hours working on analyzing the problem, a relatively unstructured presentation-cum-communication plan can significantly upset the impact of such hard work, simply because the reader (audience) of the communication does not have the patience to decipher the core message presented in a laboriously constructed treatise.

My recommendation for many aspiring business professionals would be to follow some simple rules of structuring their communication documents to make them more impactful. I have listed below some useful elements that I have picked up during my professional tenure. However, I must also caution the reader to use them judiciously and only in circumstances that a logical argument needs to be provided in a business communication context.

The three main areas that, as a communicator, one needs to pay attention to are as follows:

1. The synthesis of the communication (main message),
2. Creating a compelling structure for the communication,
3. Understanding the expectations of the audience (reader).

Synthesis

The main message of the document answers the primary question in the mind of the reader (audience) and should necessarily be articulated in the initial (first) page of the document. For maximum effectiveness of the communication, the presenter ought to have a good grasp of the primary question. In the event of a gap in the understanding, clearly the impact of the presentation will be diluted. For most audiences, this message should be simply put, terse and sufficient to answer the main concern that they may have. Suffice to say that the message ought to be long enough to comprehensively answer the overarching question, but not too long to cause disengagement with the message. A good thumb rule would be to check if the message can be stated in '30 seconds'.

Usually, the main message is a 'synthesis' of finding (an implication or a recommendation based on the findings) rather than an exposition of facts or a summary of the same. Additionally, it should provide adequate leads into the structure of the presentation.

Creating an Impactful Structure of Presentation

A well-thought-out structure helps in organizing the details of the presentation content effectively around the main message, so that the supporting arguments complement the veracity of the main message rather than create confusion. Practitioners have usually adopted the following two ways of creating effective logical structure of the presentation:

1. Top-down hierarchical structure
2. Sequenced and logical structure

Top-down Hierarchical Structure

In structuring the presentation in the top-down order, the main message is supported in such a manner that the evidence appears in the consequent hierarchical (lower) level. Usually the document layout begins with a page that answers the primary question (main message). Each subsequent layer in the pyramid is used to provide supporting evidence to the message in the layer above. Usually, up to five supporting points are used to optimally create an effective message.

This presentation format (Figure 7.1) ensures a defensible argument for all assertions made in an anticipated hierarchical manner. The value of the hierarchy is that it enables the audience (reader) to sequentially move from the essence of the document to the details and allows a premature closure of the presentation without compromising on comprehensiveness, should the reader feel that she/he does not require further factual support beyond a certain level of detail.

Sequenced and Logical Structure

This format (Figure 7.2) is useful when the argument can be posed in a logical sequence beginning with a description of the context, which provides a firm background to the presented problem that requires a business resolution. The main message is usually an emphatic reinforcement of the resolution. It is necessary to ensure a

FIGURE 7.1   Top-down Hierarchical Group—Examples

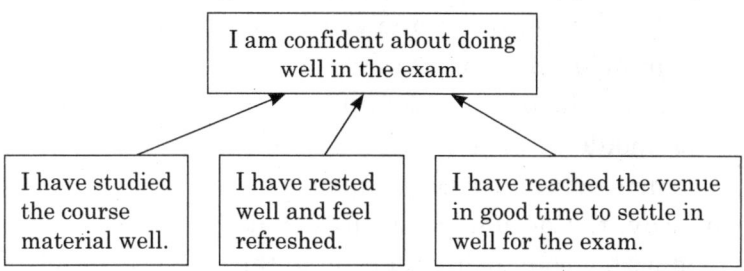

- Two to five separate but similar dimensions that answer one question per level
- Do not overlap or leave important gaps in the structure

Source: Adapted from Minto (1987).[1]

FIGURE 7.2   Sequenced and Logical Structure—An Argument Can be Impactful if It Is Done Correctly

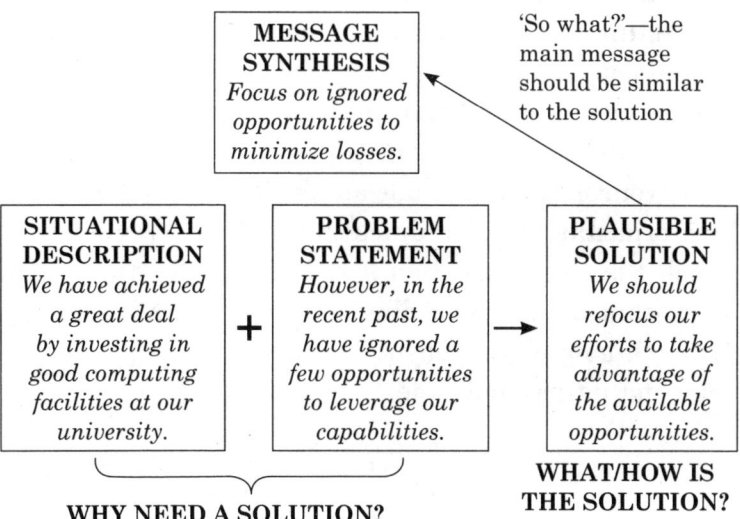

Source: Adapted from Minto (1987).[2]

---

[1]Barbara Minto, *The Pyramid Principle: Logic in Writing and Thinking* (London: Pitman Publishing, 1987).

[2]Barbara Minto, *The Pyramid Principle: Logic in Writing and Thinking* (London: Pitman Publishing, 1987), 13–77.

logical flow between the three parts to the argument, i.e. situation, complication and resolution. Specifically, the description of the context (situation) should provide logical cues for the problem definition (complication) and the latter should be so presented that arguably there can be only one resolution option, which is the one presented. In this way, the document ensures that the reader is provided with a convincing solution to the business problem being addressed.

Managing the Audience's Expectations

This should not be hard to comprehend. While I am not suggesting the presenters should 'play to the gallery', it is essential to try to get a prior notion regarding the motivations of the audience—what they might be 'looking for' and how one might 'arrest their attention'. This endeavour may also include ascertaining as to the appropriate means of communication and the frequency at which the communication should be made. Simple but significant details regarding the communication format can go a long way in ensuring the correct impact of the same, for desired outcome.

Eight

EPILOGUE

I have finally completed all significant aspects on my customized 'cook book' on business management. As parting comments, I would like to draw the reader's attention to two other areas of significance in today's management education. First, it is very crucial to state your assumptions before making an assertion. It is not enough for me to repeat myself to emphasize the importance of this comment. Management, which is largely an imperfect science, is a victim to interpretations based on many unsaid assumptions. This may be a reason why many classroom discussions continue for long hours without any possible convergence in thought. As stated earlier, for many concepts in marketing and strategy (especially), there are multiple definitions depending on the context of their usage. I have previously noted that literature has a record of multiple definitions[1] of 'brand equity'. I would guess that a classroom discussion on 'brand equity',

---

[1] Kevin Keller, 'Conceptualizing, Measuring and Managing Customer-based Brand Equity', *Journal of Marketing*, 57 (1), (January 1993): 1–22.

without adequate specificity on the context of use, may yield little logical traction in the discussion. The basis of multiple definitions of the same 'concept' is the fact that many are conjectural, especially the ones related to the 'state of mind'. A large part of management literature that deals with the psychological aspects of organizations is primarily validated by conjectural hunches and circumstantial evidences. Without the availability of hard evidencing (no one can see what is happening inside the human brain), many management concepts associated with the human psyche remain nebulous and require careful articulation, lest they are misinterpreted. This is perhaps the reason that there are few standardized definitions in management parlance.

Second, most critical decision-making require support from a well-rounded analysis using multiple approaches and information sources. In spite of the best efforts, for reasons specified previously, analyses remain imperfect and can be subject to criticism. In order to ensure the best possible support for a probable decision, it may be worthwhile to pre-empt any potential criticism of the 'plan of action' by identifying potential weaknesses due to the plausible imperfection in the analyses. In my experience, such pre-emptive approach not only attracts appreciation in a management decision-making forum, but more importantly, ensures a thorough due-diligence of potential weaknesses in the selected managerial initiative. Such discipline is necessary to provide for effective fallback measures in retrospect, in case of adverse impact of a potentially 'wrong' decision.

A FINAL WORD ON THE MOTIVATION BEHIND WRITING THIS MANUSCRIPT

I hope this manuscript has been useful in describing some aspects of management in a more simplified manner. Unfortunately, over the years, the management discipline has been labelled as being exotic and 'hard to attain'. In reality, many of the principles are pretty commonplace and ordinary, unlike the perception and the publicity the discipline has gathered.

India requires skilled managers much beyond the capacity that exists in the expanding business school landscape. While this may support the idea of opening more training institutions, I firmly believe that some of the premier institutions, which have had a head start in this arena, do not address the more basic requirements of management training required for the mass entrepreneurship in the country. Unfortunately, the latter have depended mainly on 'hand me down' business skills passed on over generations of business leaders. Additionally, the lack of academic prowess in delivering quality training at the ever-growing numbers of business schools in the country makes it difficult for needy students to imbibe sound managerial concepts.

My attempt in this treatise is to highlight the critical need to reinvent business education in order to maintain its relevance. In an era of scarcity of resources, while the premier business schools may have an important agenda to drive 'rigour', they do not address the yawning need that exists for relevant management training that is scalable, relevant and bereft of the trappings of exoticism (see Box 8.1 for an example). While this attempt at simplification is not comprehensive enough to cover all aspects of management principles, it does address the more frequently required principles of management.

BOX 8.1   Corporate Education: Strategic Investment or a Ritualistic 'Prayer'?

I have considered myself fortunate enough to be on both sides, the 'giving' and 'receiving' end of executive education—corporate training interventions that supposedly assist in developing employees for retooling and professional growth—an experience, which has been all but uneventful. I recall with some incredulity, an incident that happened to me a few years ago during a sabbatical with a business firm.

The organization hired a reputable international corporate training firm to develop its executives. The trainers had come down to our office to speak to some of us, prospective trainees, including myself. To cut to the chase, I was asked a very pointed question at the meeting for which I was totally unprepared—*so Mr Banerjee,…what are your personal training needs?*

After a brief pause while I took stock of my embarrassment, I looked helplessly at the representative from the training department of my organization and gasped, *'Please help me… am I supposed to answer this question by myself? After all, you are the guys who hired these trainers, right!!!'* Much to my dismay, the training guy from head office had no answer. He had assumed that my peers and I could articulate our training requirements, irrespective of whatever may be the corporate objective for such an intervention.

No harm though, about trainers asking their prospective audience about the latter's training needs; what was

(Box 8.1 continued)

(Box 8.1 continued)

uncharacteristic about this experience was the supposedly 'undefined' objective for corporate training, presumably because they were either not well articulated or not communicated effectively down the rank and file. Either way, it appeared downright wasteful for corporate resources to be utilized in such a manner.

This somewhat bizarre experience of mine is unfortunately typical of many corporate learning and development initiatives. To the best of my recollection, very few training initiatives that I have been associated with, as a trainer, had any concrete corporate objective. Some were focused on an event (training necessary for induction, promotion and certification of qualification), while others had very philosophical motives, which are usually hard to pinpoint—*need to equip them with tools to deal with today's liberalized and competitive environment, etc.* None had a follow-up in terms of measuring performance impact or validation of learning, although, to be exact, some made attempts, yet did not sustain. A few initiatives had a follow-up examination, but merely to improve the attention span of the participants during the program.

On an average, training requirements vary between 7 and 21 days or more per employee in most organizations. Given the significant level of commitment in executive time and resources in this effort, it is surprising that follow-up validation of training effectiveness is rarely achieved. Instead, what gets measured very often is participants' rating of the training sessions, which may not always have a direct bearing on the usefulness of the intervention. Many a time, 'well-rated' training sessions are indeed stimulating, yet participants find it difficult to articulate any tangible learning points that they can take back to their work bench.

Source: Author's own.

I must admit that I have not yet found a reasonable approach to resolving the issue of mass dissemination of the knowledge to the scale that is required in India. In our zeal to create new 'brick and mortar'—only institutions in the country to offer degree and diploma programmes in management with sparse faculty in a classroom environment—I believe we may be losing sight of the more fundamental dilemma of making management education accessible at a scale required in the country. In a society where an expanding but still very few business schools with even fewer qualified faculty offer rigorous education to a few lucky ones, I would like to think that there are plenty of opportunities for managers in the education space to provide innovative solutions for simple, relevant but widely accessible business acumen and wisdom.

Appendix

EFFECTIVE RETAIL PROMOTION MANAGEMENT

Use of POS Information Resources[1]

The use of Point of Sales (POS) data in developing analytical models that provide insights into managerial decision making in the context of retailing has been well-documented in marketing science literature. A recent article on this issue (Bucklin and Gupta, 1999) articulates the progress made in the consumer packaged goods industry in the United States in the past twenty years in harnessing POS data both in academic research as well as in developing effective industry practices in the area of retail promotion management. Some of the decision areas under retail promotions that have been extensively researched are:

1. Product pricing at retail outlets which includes decisions on timing and depth of discounts.

---

[1]Earlier appeared in the 'Vikalpa', Vol. 25, No. 4, Oct.–Dec. 2000, co-authored with Bibek Banerjee.

2. In-store display planning which includes issues on what brands/product categories to display and location of such displays.

3. In-store communication and advertising management – issues on design of ceiling signs, mobiles, inflatables, floor graphics, danglers, instant redeemable coupons etc.

4. Local area advertising decisions to promote products that build store traffic.

5. Decisions regarding shelf space allocation and arrangement of brands to command optimal visibility.

6. Decisions regarding store coupon circulation for various product categories.

India has witnessed a surge in organized retailing in the recent past. While the retailing industry is still in its infancy stage and growth opportunities are significant, the lessons from more developed markets suggest that increased competition in this area will demand better operational efficiencies to remain viable in the long run. To be able to support good decision-making for the future, retailing organizations require to equip themselves, among other things, with the infrastructure to develop and manage customer databases which can be effectively mined in the future to help drive strategy-building.

Investing in POS data has been a reasonable success story in the western markets and this paper attempts to highlight some of the plausible applications of such data. It also emphasizes the areas in which retailing majors could possibly invest to reap the benefits of market information in the future.

WHAT IS POS DATA?

As the name suggest, POS data is information collected at the retail store that provide volumetric information on every transaction made, i.e., the quantity sold, both in numbers and value, the price at which the transaction was made and any added information regarding promotional programs which the store ran at the time the transaction took place. POS provides marketers with direct behavioural information on what consumers buy.

POS data has been recorded in a systematic manner in India for over a decade now, albeit at a modest scale. ORG-MARG has an extensive operation in India that conducts a monthly retail audit on a sample of stores for a limited number of brands/Stock Keeping Units (SKU). The information recorded has been primarily volumetric data, which have been used by FMCG companies to track market share over time. While third party data collection practices at the retail store have been around for a while in India, the fragmented nature of retail industry has inhibited the collection of individual transaction level data at the retail store. With the coming of organized retailing in India in the past three to four years and its projected spiralling growth (₹160,000 crores by 2005[2]), transactional level POS data availability has been on the increase, especially with most retailing giants having electronic check out in their retail outlets which facilitate easy recording and storage of data.

---

[2]Interview with Simon Bell, Principal, AT Kearney, ET Interactive, *Economic Times*, 18 March 2000, New Delhi.

WHY IS POS DATA AN IMPORTANT SOURCE OF MANAGERIAL INFORMATION?

POS provides a rich source of behavioural data on the customers' purchase characteristics. It is the most disaggregate form of behavioural data available from the retail outlet. In comparison, the monthly retail audit data collected by ORG-MARG aggregates brand sales over a period of a month. Therefore, the details of the purchases made on every transaction are not available at this higher order of aggregation. POS data has been used to develop various analytical frameworks that have provided important insights into consumer retail purchase behaviour. In marketing science literature, a seminal paper on modelling brand choice (Guadagni and Little, 1983) with marketing mix variables using consumer panel data marked the initiation of a spate of research on consumer behaviour using panel as well as store level retail transaction data.

In the developed countries, especially in the United States, research companies such as ACNielsen and IRI have established businesses collecting both store level (POS) and consumer panel level information. The information collected is used primarily for tracking studies of market share, but over the past twelve years consumer data has been systematically analyzed to generate value added insights on consumer reaction to various marketing mix initiatives. The SCAN*PRO model (Wittink et al., 1988) and its variants have been extensively used by practising managers, especially in the packaged goods industry in the United States to develop an understanding of the causal effects of price and retail promotion. Some of the areas which have been extensively researched, both in academic institutions as well as in industry are discussed below.

Analysis of Key Drivers of Sales

Price and In-store Promotion variables have traditionally captured the attention of both retail store managers and brand managers. What brands to promote and when, for how long, which will drive profitability of the store or brand, has been of prime importance to managers in this industry in the United States for long. To evaluate the relative importance of various promotional vehicles, like temporary price reductions, coupon offers, in-store special displays, freebies, and local area feature advertising of price-offs, the SCAN*PRO model (Wittink et al., 1988) has been extensively used. Managers across various companies ranging from Kraft, Coca Cola, Pepsi and Proctor & Gamble to name a few, have used this modelling technique to examine the effect of various trade promotion initiatives. The end objective has been to develop normative models that help make decisions regarding optimal promotional spending – how much to spend, on what brand to spend and what specific promotions to run. Promotional price elasticity and base price elasticity are estimated using the SCAN*PRO model output to make pricing decisions, wherein issues regarding long term impact of price changes are weighed against short run promotional price effects.

A very effective managerial tool developed by market research organizations specializing in the retail industry using POS data has been the *Sales Rate Chart*. This is simply a distribution of sales volume generated at a retail outlet across various price points. The chart is simple but provides important information on sales spikes due to price changes. Sales rate charts have their limitations in terms of analytical rigor, however they have proven to be a successful tool in making broad pricing decisions both in the long and short run.

Analysis of Category Management Issues

Three specific decision areas that have benefited by the use of POS information analysis are:

1. Optimal product portfolio size at the retail outlet and retail shelf space optimization,
2. Optimal retail promotion initiatives to maximize retail category contribution,
3. Optimal trade allowance package to be offered to retailers by manufacturers with the objective of maximizing manufacturer's category contribution.

While the first two areas are primarily retail management issues and are of prime most importance to store managers, brand and category management specialists in manufacturing organizations are necessarily concerned about optimizing their own brand portfolio contributions. Sometimes these objectives may work against each other, for example, if promotion of brand A in the store brings in high volume share for the particular brand, which is good for the manufacturer of brand A; however, promoting brand A cannibalizes sale of other brands in the category in the retail store to such an extent that it causes a fall in the total contribution for the product category in the retail store.

With retailing dominated by large organized corporations in the United States who have the leverage to negotiate better terms with manufacturers to maintain brand visibility in the store, manufacturers have been forced to devise promotion mechanisms that harmonize retailer's category profit objectives along with their own.

In the context of using POS data for developing analytical frameworks for resolving category management issues, brand and category managers in United States have constructed causal models which determine not only the direct effect of own price and promotional mix elements on sales of the brand, but also the cross effects of marketing mix elements of other brands which are deemed to be direct competitors. Own price/promotional elasticities and cross price/promotional elasticities elements are inputs to build category profit simulators which are typically scenario building tools which help in designing effective promotional programs which maximize contribution.

Such exercises are carried out quite regularly at large packaged goods companies. In the beer category, extensive use of this simulator has been made by the second largest brewery in the US market. The specific purpose of this project has been to convince retailers across the US markets that promoting their brand of beer on key holiday weeks maximize profits for the retailers compared to promoting the market leader brand.

Rationalizing on portfolio and shelf space management requires additional inputs in terms of layout design of retail stores (planograms) which when integrated with

POS sales information can provide significant insights into optimal portfolio size as well as the area and shelf location to be allotted to different product categories with the objective to maximize the retail sales or profits. Exercises of this nature are performed regularly with fair degree of success in developing appropriate marketing decisions. Several research companies have developed syndicated analytical models which have had limited success in resolving issues across the board. They go by nomenclature such as Portfolio Manager or Category Manager, however based on our experience, developing customized solutions using POS data have had significant potential in resolving product assortment and shelf space management issues.

Advertising

The use of POS data along with media exposure data as collected by research agencies in the US, such as Nielsen Media Research (ORG-MARG collects media exposure data in India) have been used by brand managers to calibrate their long term advertising spendings. There have been attempts at studying the short-term effects of advertising on sales, however the impacts estimated have been fairly low (0.1 to 0.12 for established brands, 0.2 to 0.4 for new brands). There has been moderate success at estimating advertising impact on sales in the long run (1.5 to 2 times more than short run effects).

An explanation for these lukewarm results may rest with the characteristics of data resources used to construct the analysis. Research agencies such as ACNielsen and IRI favour the use of store level data (POS) to study advertising effects, which they claim is consistent with the analysis conducted to study the effect of store promotions (Bucklin and Gupta, 1999). This point is however debatable since other agencies (presumably not having access to store level data) have argued for the appropriateness of using market level data to estimate the impact of what they call market-level phenomenon such as advertising. Readers should note that market level sales data is obtained by aggregating POS data across all stores in a market over an appropriate time window. Using appropriate projection factors that account for the population of stores can also use sample data collected by ORG across stores to estimate market level data.

While brand managers are concerned about the effectiveness of their advertising budget, retail managers also need to know about the impact of advertising on brands, especially advertising campaigns of new brands and new product categories.

THE RETAILING ENVIRONMENT IN INDIA

With her population touching a billion, India is working at the doorsteps of becoming one of the world's foremost consumer markets. About a quarter of this huge mass of consumers live in towns and cities and the remaining in villages. Over the years, the retailing infrastructure that has proliferated in India is characterized by a high degree of fragmentation as compared to many developed nations. A recent estimate puts the figure at 10 million operational retail outlets in India, 32% of these being in urban areas. Small stores (about 300–400 sq. ft.) accounted for 64% of the retail outlets in the country whereas very large stores (about 800 sq. ft.) constituted only 3% of the establishments. FMCG stores accounted for nearly 75% of these retail outlets. According to a CMIE[3] forecast, total retail sales in India is likely to exceed ₹9200 billion by the year 2002, of which about 73% is expected in the food sector. Therefore, it is but obvious that the great Indian retailing revolution is not, at the least, waiting for the size of the business opportunity. The challenge lies in identifying the key drivers that steer the Indian consumers' perception and behaviour when it comes to her shopping needs.

In this context, market enthusiasts are crystal gazing on the 'fate' of large format and/or organised retailing in India. There are interesting trends by way of statistics, e.g. the friendly neighbourhood mom & pop stores have increased per 1000 population as per an ORG study, and large format and specialty retailing is also on the increase (though their absolute members are yet quite small). All this at the expense of perhaps the middle-sized-middle-value shops.[4] The reality is that every retailer has to "understand his customers" more discerningly than ever before and make strategic choices to pursue the right target (customer) with the right proposition. Also, the reality is that every retailer today is unanimous in their appreciation that they need to "deliver value" to their customers.

The final reality is that in today's retailing environment in India the sheer complexity of the product-market matrix is posing 'mental-model' based decision making a

---

[3]Centre for Monitoring Indian Economy.

[4]Hindu Business Line, 'Responding to Modern retailing Formats', The Hindu Business Line, 23 May 1998.

real challenge. This exponential change started during the early 90s, essentially from two sources. First, in pursuit of the proverbial 200 million strong Indian middle class the manufacturers have been continually adding new products in the market place. For instance, in the FMCG sector, there were 57 core categories of products in 1990, which grew to 76 by 1996 (and the trend continues). These 19 new categories boasted of 1378 brands and 2579 stock keeping units (SKUs). Furthermore, the number of SKUs in the erstwhile 57 categories also grew from 7,715 to 15,160 during the same period (Banerjee et al., 1999).

The second change agent, and the most important, is the consumer who has become vastly discerning through her rapid exposure to the global business environment. The Indian consumer today reflects a strong preference for imperatives such as evaluating choices from among large assortments of products, a pleasurable shopping experience, and a shopping experience that provided her the maximum "value" per rupee spent.

Herein lies the opportunity of utilizing the POS data to model consumer response to marketing mix variables at the retail level. With increasing competition, both at the manufacturer level and at the retail level, it is obvious that there are distinct advantages of being the first mover in harnessing information resources to drive the marketing strategy building exercise, both for retailers and manufacturers. The latter will increasingly feel the pressure of building strategies that are in congruence with the retailers' business objectives.

The rapid changes in the retailing environment are currently quite evident at least in some of the metropolitan pockets of the country. A fairly extensive review of the expanding retailing sector in India is available in prominent trade publications.[5] Competition has set in from multiple sources. In the Chennai market, competition in food retailing is multi faceted with the neighbourhood stores (kirana) facing direct competition from more than one organized retailing chains: FoodWorld, Nilgiri's, Subhiksha and Vitan. With such intense competition in the market, newer retailing chains are forced to adopt significantly differentiated POS strategy to make customers change their shopping habits. For instance, the specific trade publication reports that Subhiksha adopts a blanket policy of discounting prices by selling less than MRP, similar to the textbook definition of an Everyday Low Pricing (EDLP) strategy. "You have to give customers a solid reason to change their shopping behaviour. One which conventional stores like the kirana can't duplicate", says the director of Subhiksha chain of supermarkets.

The above instance corroborates our assertion that retailers of the future will have to rapidly employ differentiated marketing strategy based on customer response information. Utilizing customer behaviour data at Point of Sale to develop effective pricing strategies, EDLP or otherwise, will certainly be the imperative for long term survival and growth.

STATUS OF POS DATA IN RETAIL MANAGEMENT IN INDIA

As was pointed out earlier, ORG-MARG has operated a retail store audit in India for many years. The data

---

[5]*Brand Equity, Economic Times*, 26 April–2 May 2000.

primarily consists of actual stock movement data at sample stores. Collection of corresponding marketing mix elements has been minimal, and only very recently some effort has been made to collect price and promotion data. ACNielsen is also reported to be planning to develop an audit infrastructure. However, none of these organizations are capable of fully collating the rich transaction level data that exists at the retail point of sales. ACNielsen and IRI claim to provide census data on store sales, but only in few geographic regions in the United States.

A typical source of POS transactional data will have information on the following:

1. Wider range of SKUs (Stock Keeping Units).
2. Tracking of generic/store brand sales.
3. Ability to handle consumer panels through loyalty programs.
4. Ability to conduct product basket analysis.
5. Ability to generate information on optimal "loss leader" promotion strategy.

A recent study document prepared on this topic (Raghuram et al., 1999) highlights some of the analytical capabilities of this type of information. However, a detailed assessment of a typical POS transactional level database available today shows the limited amount of information collected currently (Box A.1). This is not surprising given that use of the data has been primarily to generate simple accounting reports. In order to develop the full potential of POS data for decision making, the future managers have to proactively think of information

BOX A.1   Type of POS Data Available

- Item Files
  - o Bill Date, Bill Number, Bill Time, Product Code, Cost, MRP, Sold Value, Quantity
- Product Master
  - o Product Code, Product Name, MRP, Group Code
- Group Master
  - o Group Code, Group Name
- Campaign Files
  - o Product Code, Campaign Start Date, Campaign End Date, Cost, MRP, Selling Price, Campaign Number

Source: Raghuram et al. (1999).

bytes that need to be systematically collected which can be used along with the transaction level data in the future to help making better store level decisions.

One area that conventional grocery stores like the small kirana stores cannot replicate is the investment in infrastructure that organized retailing chains have made in collecting transaction level data. An ad hoc survey in the Ahmedabad market, which is in the infancy stage of the retailing revolution compared to its counterparts in the south, revealed that a significant number of super-market stores collected transaction data at the cash register. Yet, no significant efforts are made currently to "mine" this database to reveal insights on customer behaviour. Even with limited information availability, these databases have enough data to understand market-level drivers of store sales. The reasons for this perceived apathy may be varied; lack of expertise in mining data may be an important reason but more often it is the issue of prioritization of initiatives that has kept developmental projects such as database mining a back burner. This is most unfortunate since we predict that with rapid entry of competition, players who understand customer psyche, through its manifestation of overt behaviour will dictate the future course of the retailing industry.

AN EXAMPLE OF A POTENTIAL ANALYSIS

We used a database obtained from a store of a large retail food chain based in South India to identify specific "category-driven" transactions that generate more revenue for the store. The purpose of the study was to identify customer segments that on an average generated more revenue for the store compared to others. Customer segments were identified based on their main purchase category as exhibited by the nature of their transaction.

Transaction data over a four-month time period across all recorded product categories in the store were used for the analysis. Five major category purchases were identified for the study based on the frequency of purchases made (weighted by the value of the purchase). These categories were: *(a)* staple, *(b)* spices, *(c)* cooking oils, *(d)* pulses and *(e)* toilet soap. A sixth category was formed clubbing sales from all other categories. The number of categories chosen for the study was kept at six to avoid unnecessarily complicating the study, but the analysis can be done at any level of detail. It must be pointed out that while this type of data has been available in India only in the past three to four years, currently there does not seem to be a scarcity of transaction data in electronic form in the organized retailing sector.

Due to the paucity of data, each individual transaction in the store (identified as all purchases made during one store visit based on a unique bill number) was categorized as either a particular category driven purchase or not (e.g. staple driven purchase or not staple driven purchase) based on the rupee value spent on the category in the specific transaction. To control for variation in average value spent across categories, the purchases were categorized based on their relative value compared to the maximum value recorded in that category across the entire database. This is a limitation, since without any customer-related characteristics in the database, it is impossible to identify the drivers of individual purchases and hence one has to resort to approximations.

SAS software was used to manipulate the data and the results obtained are presented in Table A.1. The direct interpretation of the results is that customers that came into the store primarily to buy staples spent on an average ₹517 compared to customers who did not have staples as a major category in their shopping list

TABLE A.1   Average Transaction Value (in ₹)

Category	Key Purchase[1]	Minor Purchase
Staple	517	160
Spices	445	130
Cooking Oils	620	153
Pulses	556	140
Soap	475	152

Note: [1] When the key purchase is of the corresponding category.

(average spending per transaction is ₹160). Similarly, the average transaction, which was driven by spice purchase, was valued at ₹445 compared to ₹130 that was spent by customers who did not have spices as a major category in their shopping list.

The largest difference in the transaction value occurs between transactions that record significant purchase of cooking oils versus the transactions that do not record significant purchases of cooking oil (₹620 vs ₹153).

This result throws some light on the type of customers that bring in more value to the store in terms of revenue (refer Chen et al., 1999). If store managers were to make decisions about promotions in the local area to draw more customers, the typical output obtained from this analysis may be used to identify the "right" destination category to be featured in the local area promotion to increase store traffic of high valued customers. In the present case, high propensity of using cooking oil as a promotion category will attract the highest revenue customer.

DESIGNING PROPER INFORMATION RESOURCE TO HELP BETTER DECISION-MAKING: THE INDIAN CONTEXT

There are limitations in the analysis described above given the approximations made in categorizing transactions into specific category driven purchases due to the lack of customer descriptors. Also, the results obtained are not statistically robust enough to pass a test of technical rigor. Although, technical rigor is needed, but often-times appropriate data analysis (even without passing the litmus test) provides a higher level understanding of consumer behaviour which can shape better decision making. What is critical to drive the process is availability of the right information/data resource that can be mined. In this respect FoodWorld (C) (refer Banerjee et al., 1999) touches on the need to "IT-enable" operations for smooth running of the retail operations. We would suggest that retail organizations of the future do need to go beyond envisioning IT integration. They will benefit by adopting a proactive stance in designing and developing an IT enabled information warehouse for both customer and operational information, which can significantly drive strategic decision making in the future. As a starting point, an assessment of the type of decisions that one needs to take in more advanced stages of the business life cycle is necessary. Lessons from the developed markets of the west and the type of decision problems that they have faced may provide leads to the type of information requirements of the future.

SOME BROAD LEVEL INITIATIVES

Initiating customer loyalty programs is a pragmatic way of collating customer level transactional data that can be linked to customer characteristics. Segment level analysis of customer likes and dislikes drive most marketing decision making and this type of database provides ample opportunity to hone in-store promotional programs based on the type of customers who frequent the store. An effective way of utilizing this behavioural information is to generate customized coupons and promotional features at the checkout counters based on the customer characteristics and current purchases made. Catalina Corporation, a Chicago based research agency has evolved such coupon generating machines that have been set up at several retail food stores across the United States. Manufacturers have also availed of this service at retail counters to induce brand switching with limited success. However, the true value of this loyalty program is to provide individualized promotions to customers, which enhances perceived service quality at the store.

There are a number of non-food departmental store chains in Mumbai and Delhi, who have introduced loyalty programs and are tracking purchase data on these customers. Proper design and mining of these databases can yield significant insights to develop direct mail promotion campaigns.

There is tremendous opportunity to enhance the scope of in-store promotions and to capture the information at the most disaggregate level. In-store displays whether they are end of aisle displays, within aisle or front of store have been recorded to have varying effects on sale spikes. A deeper understanding of the drivers of in-store sales will help retail store managers plan their space utilization more effectively in conjunction with the most appropriate marketing program. It is important to invest in an initial period of testing various innovative marketing options and recording them religiously, such as one would do in conducting pilot test program. After the initial phase of testing, managers would have a sufficiently large information base to fine tune their programs according to the market needs. However, this latter stage does make the database created redundant. Effective ongoing decision making demands continuous building and mining databases as well.

CONCLUSIONS

Retailing is entering an active phase in its business life-cycle in India. This paper has attempted to address a dimension of this business, which has a strategic role to play in the growth and development of its constituents—the management of information resource. Like many other service industries which has become intensely focussed on information resource management, for example, consumer finance, insurance and hospitality, survival in the long run will depend upon smart management of market information resources. Unfortunately, developing marketing information resources need a significant lead-time and there is a natural advantage of being the first off the block. Large retail chains have a definite advantage with respect to the available infrastructure that they have in place. They simply have to initiate a proactive process of investing in the appropriate information that will yield the right kind of marketing insight for the future.

REFERENCES

Banerjee, Bibek, G. Raghuram, Abraham Koshy, (1999), FoodWorld (C), The Road Ahead, Indian Institute of Management, Ahmedabad, India.

Bucklin, Randolph, Sunil Gupta, (1999), Commercial Use of UPC Scanner Data: Industry and Academic Perspectives, *Marketing Science*, Vol. 18, No. 3, pp. 247-273.

Chen, Yuxin, James D. Hess, Ronald T. Wilcox, Z. John Zhang, (1999), Accounting Profits Vs Marketing Profits: A relevant Metric for Category Management, *Marketing Science*, Vol. 18, No. 3, pp. 208-229.

Raghuram,G., Bibek Banerjee, A.K. Jain, Abraham Koshy, Gunjan Bhatt, (1999), Retailscope '99, Retail Sales Data: The Hidden Treasure, Draft Report, Indian Institute of Management, Ahmedabad 380015.

Guadagni, Peter M., John D.C. Little, (1983), A Logit Model of Brand Choice calibrated on Scanner Data, *Marketing Science*, 2(Summer), pp. 203-238.

Wittink, Dick R., Michael Addona, William Hawkes, John Porter, (1988), SCAN*PRO: the estimation, validation and use of promotional effects based on scanner data. Working paper, AC Nielsen, Schaumburg, IL.

ABOUT THE AUTHOR

Arindam Banerjee joined the faculty at IIM Ahmedabad after working in the industry for over seven years. After securing his PhD in Marketing Sciences, Professor Banerjee was associated with various consulting/market research firms in the United States. During his tenure in industry, he worked on business analytics problems in the Retail Financial Services, FMCG/Retail and the Consumer Durable sectors. He has consulted with GE Capital, Sears Roebuck, Bank One, Miller Brewing Company, Kraft Foods and Chase Manhattan Bank, among others.

In the past 14 years at IIM Ahmedabad, he has worked on consulting and training assignments with a number of Indian and multinational companies based in India such as Hindustan Unilever Limited, the TATA Group, TVS Group, Infosys Technologies, Genpact, Household Finance Corporation (HSBC North America), Monsanto India, PepsiCo India, Ericsson (India) Pvt. Ltd., and the Coffee Board (Government of India). He has helped in developing marketing and business strategy for Indian companies coping up with the recent liberalized and competitive environment. He has also worked on building specific systems and internal processes to reinforce fact-based business decision-making in many organizations. These engagements have typically included a mix of process design, implementation, and training of internal personnel in managing them. In 2006–2007, he worked full-time for HSBC Global Services in Bangalore (on leave from IIMA) to build and lead an offshore analytics team to support the bank's business in the United States.

He has also published extensively in national and international academic journals in management such as the *Journal of Segmentation in Marketing, International Journal of Retail and Distribution Management, International Journal of Management and Decision Making, Asia-Pacific Journal of Marketing and Logistics, Strategic Outsourcing, Vikalpa* and the *Decision*. Besides, he has written five cases in the area of fact-based decision-making and strategy. A few of his articles on effective business practices have appeared in trade publications such as the *Indian Management* and *Hindustan Times*.

Prior to joining the IIM, he was a senior consultant at Mitchell Madison Group, a global management consultancy firm, based at their Chicago office. Previously, he has headed the marketing analytics team at ACNielsen Corporation in Chicago, providing consulting services to some of the Philip Morris Group of Companies. He is a Professor of Marketing and Quantitative Methods at IIM Ahmedabad.